AMERICAN
SOLDIERS
OF THE
REVOLUTION

Alan Kemp

ALMARK PUBLISHING CO. LTD., LONDON

First Published—February 1972

ISBN 0 85524 058 X (hard cover edition)
ISBN 0 85524 059 8 (paper covered edition)

Printed in Great Britain by
Vale Press Ltd., Mitcham, Surrey, CR4 4HR
for the publishers, Almark Publishing Co. Ltd.,
270 Burlington Road, New Malden,
Surrey, KT3 4NL, England

Introduction

IT appears strange to many students of the American Revolution how a regular British force, made up of some of Europe's finest soldiers, could suffer so harshly at the hands of the motley collection of farmers and artisans who took up arms against the Crown in 1775.

On the face of it the conflict takes on the atmosphere of a David and Goliath confrontation, with John Bull's Goliath, disciplined and professionally schooled in the art of musket and bayonet, falling to the Colonists' David armed with no more than a hunting rifle and a ploughshare sword.

The scarlet phalanxes of Minden and Fontenoy, however, were ill-suited to fighting under the conditions prevailing in the New World. This was shown on the first day of the War when the British suffered almost 250 casualties from the sniping American Militiamen between Lexington and Concord.

The American had certain points in his favour. To begin with, he was fighting on his home ground and took full advantage of the fact. He employed the sharp-shooting tactics he had learned in the French and Indian wars and rarely gave his opponents the opportunity of a pitched battle. Coupled with this guerrilla method of warfare was the Colonist's familiarity with firearms and the incentive that he was fighting for his freedom. He cared little for the accepted conventions of 'civilised' warfare, such as the practice of ceasing hostilities at the end of a year and going into quarters for the winter months. The surprise victory of Washington, defeating the ill-prepared Hessians at Trenton is evidence of this. Conversely, had the British come out of quarters to attack the ill-equipped Americans at Valley Forge in 1777, Lord Howe could probably have crushed the rebellion there and then.

These factors and others, such as the British Army's difficulties of supply and the frequent mishandling of its administration, put victory well within the reach of the Americans. There is a strong possibility that Independence would have been secured even without the intervention of their French allies in 1778.

When the American colonists took up arms, there could hardly have been any two of their soldiers dressed alike. Most of the Patriots answered the call dressed in everyday working or hunting clothes and armed with whatever weapons came to hand. As the conflict progressed, dress regulations were laid down and the Army took on a more soldier-like appearance. The intentions of Congress, however, were never consolidated and the fact that supply and administrative deficiencies prevented the Americans from ever presenting a totally uniformed force makes a fascinating study.

The first part of this book presents a comprehensive survey of the dress and equipment of the Patriot soldier, both uniform and utility,

and shows to some extent how he drilled and fought. Part Two of the book is devoted to the other Americans; the 50,000 Tories whose loyalty to the Crown prompted them to raise their own regiments and fight their fellow countrymen in support of the British. In compiling this work I have drawn, not only from official sources of information, such as Congressional Papers, but also from contemporary observers who recorded in words and pictures how the soldiers of the American Revolution appeared.

My thanks go to my wife who typed the manuscript from my hand written notes. The old engravings included in this volume are by courtesy of A. H. Bowling and are from his personal collection.

CONTENTS

OPPOSITE: At the Battle of Cowpens on January 17, 1781, a British and Loyalist force under Tarleton was defeated by Daniel Morgan's Militia and a small number of Patriot cavalry under William Washington. During the battle Tarleton reputedly fought a personal combat with William Washington. The British cavalry included both 17th Light Dragoons and Tarleton's Legion. In this print, Tarleton on the left, is shown wearing the uniform of the 17th Light Dragoons rather than the green of his own Legion.

FRONT COVER: A Right Company man of the Pennsylvania Line.

Minutemen
1775

Part One
THE PATRIOTS

1: Infantry

ON April 23, 1775, only four days after 'the shot heard round the world' started the War of Independence at Lexington, the Provincial Congress authorised the raising of 1,300 men. Artemas Ward was made Commander-in-Chief and an appeal was sent out to the other colonies for assistance.

In June of the same year the Continental Congress replaced Ward with George Washington as Commander-in-Chief and called for the formation of eight companies of riflemen from Pennsylvania and two each from Maryland and Virginia. This force became the 1st Continental Regiment of Infantry. It was hoped to form a strong Continental Army made up from volunteers of the best of the State Militia and soon over thirty more Continental regiments were formed. The purpose of establishing these regiments was for the men to serve the union of the states rather than merely their own colony. Each state was still responsible for organising and officering the regiments, although they were to operate on Continental service.

Throughout the War there was little consistency in the number of men in a regiment. Washington was rarely guaranteed units up to full strength due to desertion, rebellion and sickness. At this period a regiment was made up of between 400 and 700 men and for tactical purposes was called a battalion. Washington organised three divisions of two brigades each, the brigades usually containing six regiments each. In the field the Army was employed only in battalion strength; the manoeuvring of whole brigades and divisions in war had yet to be introduced.

In 1775, a regiment was composed of ten companies, each consisting of one captain, three lieutenants, four sergeants, four corporals, one drummer and about seventy privates. In 1776 the 28 regiments called for by Congress were to be made up of eight companies each. A company was to consist of one captain, two lieutenants, one ensign, four sergeants, four corporals, two drummers and fifers and 76 privates. It was just after this that Washington encouraged the formation of Light Infantry companies for his regiments; specialist troops serving as scouts and skirmishers. On certain occasions these Light Infantry companies would be gathered together from various regiments to form an elite battalion.

Later in 1776 it was decreed that 88 regiments should be raised but this was never realised. The number of men in Washington's force was now about 20,000 formed into 26 regiments of approximately 730 men each, a regiment being made up of eight companies. Sixteen of the regiments came from Massachusetts, five from Connecticut, three from New Hampshire and two from Rhode Island. The Pennsylvania Rifle Battalion was organised as an additional unit and the Artillery as another. Only one year later, after the disastrous winter at Valley Forge, Washington controlled a mere 4,000 men.

After 1778 the Americans had just under 10,000 Continental soldiers and managed to form 80 regiments in 1779 and 58 in 1781 (49 Infantry, four Cavalry, four Artillery and one Artillery Artificers). Those fluctuations in numbers continued right up to the end of the War when Congress reduced the total strength of all American forces to only eighty men in 1784.

The majority of Patriots on Continental service preferred short term enlistments, usually for one year but sometimes as little as three months. When this period was up, many left their regiments, and returned to their homes to resume the farming or whatever business they were neglecting. A private soldier was entitled to about six and a half dollars a month but pay was usually in Continental paper money which was of little real value due to inflation and rising prices. For all their patriotic zeal the men had a deep-rooted allegiance to their own state and often refused to obey officers from other colonies. Even their own officers could experience difficulty in controlling the soldiers if, for instance, the private was a neighbour of that officer and regarded him as an equal, or even more common, just did not like him! This individuality and independent streak in the men continually frustrated Washington in his efforts to establish an army on the disciplined lines of a European force. The colonial soldier was easily affected by the fortunes of war and could lose morale very quickly if conditions were not in his favour. Early in 1781, pay disputes and inadequate food and clothing caused mutinies among some of the Pennsylvania and New Jersey regiments and several executions resulted.

After the undisciplined performance of his army in the early years of the War, Washington realised that if any solidarity was to be maintained within his forces then they must be shaped by conventional methods. To do this he appointed 'Baron' von Steuben, a Prussian who had served in the army of Frederick the Great. Steuben was made Inspector General of the Army in 1778. He found that up till that time there had been no regulation drill in the American regiments, with officers using manuals of a number of different European armies.

Steuben introduced a simplified version of the Prussian drill manual and instructed selected officers in the refinements of drilling and marching procedures. These officers, in turn, went on to instruct the troops. Under the new regulations the administrative regiment ceased to be the same as the tactical battalion, which it had been in the past. Men were drilled in bodies of about 200 which afforded greater freedom of movement than before. Regiments were divided into eight companies with each company made up of two sections or platoons. The most experienced officers were assigned to the flank companies. The antiquated system of marching strung out in Indian file was abandoned and the ranks closed up to march in columns of four. Despite these improvements in regimental organisation Congress was not always forthcoming with sufficient finance for the Army and Steuben's innovations suffered because of this. The roots of his directions had taken hold however, and a new American Army was in the making.

Throughout the War, the Continental Army was supplemented by a great number of Provincial Militia units and these troops often fought well alongside the regulars. In a number of cases however certain bodies of Militiamen were found to be unreliable and for this reason Washington could never confidently depend upon them and whenever possible avoided deploying them in pitched battles with the British.

Reading the Declaration of Independence to the Army on July 9, 1776. The engraving is not entirely reliable, but does show one or two factual points such as the habit of wearing the waistbelt over the coat (Infantry in background); the coat lace sometimes adopted by musicians and the dragoon's short cut jacket of the type often preferred by mounted troops.

2: Dress of the Infantry

THE Militia and Minutemen who rallied at Lexington and Concord in 1775 were, in the main, dressed in civilian or hunting clothes. Old records of Woodbury, Connecticut, tell us that, 'The Militia rallied in whatever clothing they had. Small clothes coming down and fastening just below the knee and long stockings with cowhide shoes ornamented with large buckles . . . . Coats and waistcoats were loose and of huge dimensions with various colours and shirts made of flax and homespun

TYPES OF PATRIOT HEADGEAR.

a. The Cocked Hat (not always edged with braid).

b. Knitted Liberty Cap, usually red.

c. Cloth Liberty Cap. A variety of slogans were painted or embroidered on the front flap.

d. The Round Hat. Morgan's Rifles usually pinned this up on the left side. Thompson's Pennsylvania Rifles are usually portrayed with their hats pinned on the right.

e. The Canadian Cap. Made of wool or leather and trimmed with fur, the cap often had a fur tail hanging behind.

f. The Flopped Hat. These were made with both round and sugar-loaf crowns.

like the rest of the dress. Hats were large, round-top and broad brimmed—Weapons assorted. Occasionally a bayonet might be seen and powder horns were evident.'

Any uniforms which did appear at the onset of the War would be those of the many independent companies which existed throughout the various colonies. Sometimes the red uniforms of some State Governor's Bodyguards bore a dangerous resemblance to the coats of the British soldiers, eg, 1st Company Governor's Foot Guards of Connecticut.

At Bunker Hill on June 17, 1775, much civilian clothing was again in evidence and there was little uniformity in the military dress that did appear. A small number of Provincials were in uniform; one authority states that some New Jersey Infantry appeared in blue coats faced with red but this is not certain. More likely was the presence of the Wethersfield Company of Connecticut dressed in blue coats faced with red. Trumbull's painting of Bunker Hill shows a colonist wearing a coat of these colours. Some of the Connecticut men supposedly covered their uniforms with hunting shirts to appear less conspicuous in the action.

The Provinces now set about establishing some sort of uniformity for their soldiers but, as usual, they were working independently of each other and without any real direction. The Massachusetts Provincial Congress in July 1775 resolved 'That 13,000 coats be provided . . . and one thereof given to each non-commissioned officer and soldier of the Massachusetts forces'. They further resolved 'That each coat be faced with same kind of cloth with which it is made, that the coats be made in the common plain way, without lappels, short and with small folds'. Coats were to be fitted with pewter buttons, each regiment having its own number stamped upon them. New York was also attempting some standardisation, resolving 'That when the Green Mountain boys are raised, each of them shall be furnished with a coat and . . . be requested to furnish green cloth for the purpose and red cloth sufficient to face the coats'. (New York Provincial Congress, August 15, 1775).

TYPICAL PATRIOT BUTTONS.
a. Continental Army. Worn by Artillery as well as Infantry.
b. Continental Artillery.
c. Pennsylvania State Regt.
d. Bone or wood button worn by many troops.
e. 14th Connecticut Regt. (Burrell's).

In November of this year brown was ordered by Congress to be the recommended colour for regimental coats. This was because brown dye was available on practically every farm and cloth merchants would be able to supply the necessary quantities of material at short notice.

Even here uniformity was never complete, with many different shades of brown being seen even within the same company. The regiments were to be distinguished by the colours of their facings. As in the British Army, the new clothing was to be paid for by stoppages from the soldiers' pay. For all this attempt at uniformity many regiments were still obliged to wear whatever uniforms were available. Washington made another attempt at standardisation for his regiments in General Orders of November 13, 1775:

'The Colonels upon the new establishment to settle as soon as possible with the Quarter Master General the uniforms of their respective regiments, that the buttons may be properly numbered and work finished without delay'.

It was soon found that the most practical mode of dress was a suit of buckskins. This costume had been worn in America for reasons of availability and utility from the beginning of the War but now it was officially encouraged by the Commander-in-Chief. He instructed that 'Indian boots or leggings be provided for the men instead of stockings and that each man be given a hunting shirt'. The soldiers of the 1st Virginia Regiment of Infantry were in 1775 'Uniformed at their own expense in hunting shirts, leggings and white braiding on their hats'. One year later Washington pointed out the advantages of buckskin dress in a General Order of July 24, 1776:

'No dress can be cheaper, nor more convenient, as the wearer may be cool in warm weather and warm in cool weather by putting on undercloaths which will not change the outward dress, winter or summer . . . . Besides which it is a dress justly supposed to carry no small terror to the enemy who think every such person a complete marksman'.

In October, 1776 Congress listed the annual issue for each soldier as, 'Two linen hunting shirts, two pairs of overalls, a leather or woollen waistcoat with sleeves, one pair of breeches, a hat or leather cap, two shirts, two pairs of hose and two pairs of shoes'.

New resolutions of March 1779 again laid emphasis on uniform clothing with regard to colours of facings. Congress authorised the Commander-in-Chief, 'according to circumstances of supplies of clothing to fix and prescribe the uniform as well as with regard to colour and facings as to the cut or fashion of the clothes to be worn by the troops of the respective States and Regiments'. It further recommended,' . . . woollen overalls for winter and linen for summer to be substituted for the breeches'. A General Order issued on October 2, 1779, stated, 'The following are the uniforms that have been determined for the troops of these States respectively, as soon as the state of the public supplies will permit of their being finished accordingly; and in the meantime, it is recommended to the Officers to endeavour to accommodate their uniforms to the standard, that when the men come to be supplied, there may be a proper uniformity'. The colours decided upon for Infantry were as follows:

Regiments from New Hampshire, Massachusetts, Rhode Island and Connecticut were to wear blue coats faced white with white buttons and linings. Regiments from New York and New Jersey were to wear blue coats faced buff with white buttons and linings.

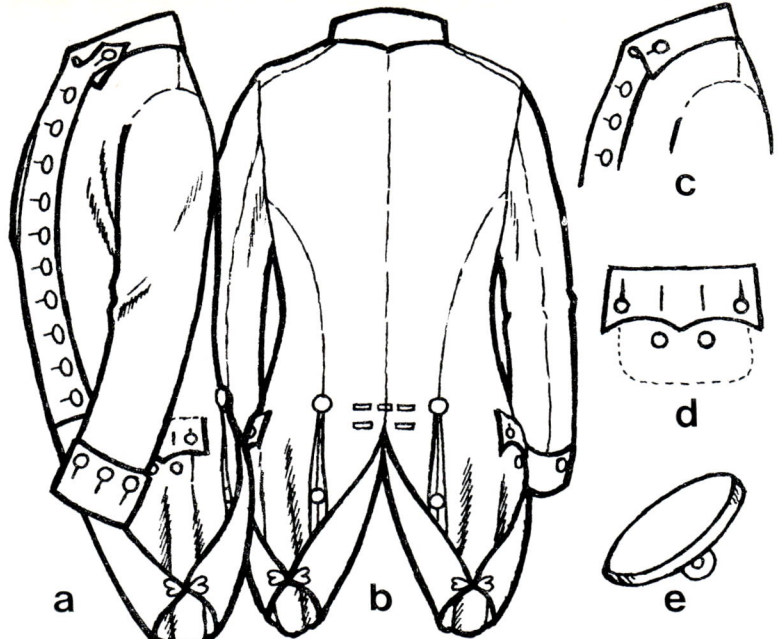

REGIMENTAL COAT OF CONTINENTAL INFANTRY.

a. and b. Side and rear views.

c. Lapel point fastened under collar.

d. Pocket flap. (Two inner buttonholes were closed).

e. Typical flat button.

The coat was made of broad cloth with linen lining and stiffened facings.

Regiments from Pennsylvania, Delaware, Maryland and Virginia were to wear blue coats faced red with white buttons and linings.

Regiments from North Carolina, South Carolina and Georgia were to wear blue coats faced lighter blue, buttonholes edged with narrow white tape or lace and with white buttons and linings.

Washington never ceased to strive for uniformity despite the setbacks of desperate supplies. He seems to have been most concerned as to how his Army appeared to foreign corps and constantly urged his officers to conform to the states pattern of coat and to pay strict attention to rank badges. (Headquarters, Totoway, November 15, 1780).

An order of 1781 gives a clear picture of the cut of this uniform:

'The length of the coat, to the upper part of the knee-pan, and to be cut high in the neck. As three is to five, so is the skirt to the waist of the coat; or divide the whole length of the coat into eight equal parts, take five for the waist and three for the skirts. The lappel at the top of the breast, to be 3 inches wide and the bottom 2 and 3/10th inches; the lappel to be as low as the waist, and its wing to button within an inch of the shoulder seam with a small button on the cape (collar). The epaulette to be worn directly on the top of the shoulder joint on the same button with the wing of the lappel. A round and close cuff, 3 inches wide, with four close-worked buttonholes. The cape to be made with a peak behind and its width in proportion to the lappels. The pocket flaps to be scolloped, four buttonholes, the two inner close-worked, the two outer open-worked, and to be set on in a curved line from the bottom of the lappel to the button on the hip. The coat to be cut full behind, with a fold on each back skirt and two close-worked buttonholes on each. Ten open-worked buttonholes on the breast of each lappel, with ten large buttons at equal distance; four large buttons on each cuff; four on each pocket-flap and four on each fold. Those on the cuffs and pocket flaps to be placed agreeable to the buttonholes; and those on the folds are on the hip, one at the bottom and two in the centre, at an equal distance with those on the lappel. The coat is to button or hook low at the fourth buttonhole on the breast and is to be flaunt at the bottom with a genteel and military air. Four hooks and eyes on the breast, as low as the coat is allowed to button. The skirts to hook up with a blue heart at each corner with such device as the Field Officers of each Regiment shall direct. The bottom of the coat to be cut square. The waistcoat to be single breasted with twelve buttons and holes on the breast, with pocket flaps, four close-worked buttonholes and four buttons, which shall appear below the flaps. The breeches are to be made with a half-fall, four buttons on each knee. The small buttons on the waistcoat to be of the same kind with the large ones on the coat. The number of the Regiment is to be in the centre of the button with such device as the Field Officers shall direct. The epaulettes to be worn agreeable to His Excellency the Commander-in-Chief's orders of June 18th, 1780. A fashionable military cock'd hat with a silver button loop and a small button with the number of the Regiment. To wear a black stock when on duty and on the parade. No edging, vellum lace, or indeed any other ornaments which are not mentioned to be added to the uniform. No officer is to be permitted, at any time, to wear any other uniform than that of his Regiment.'

Although this directive apparently refers to officers' uniforms, the appearance of the coat would be much the same for the men except, of course, without the rank refinements and probably of a coarser material.

It was decided in December 1782 that in future red should be the colour for the facings of all Infantry regiments, but again supplies of cloth failed to materialise and the following order resulted:

'The non-arrival of the clothing imported from Europe render the greatest economy in that article doubly necessary. The Commander-in-Chief recommends turning and repairing of coats of primary importance and points out that they should be shorter than at present, established by the Commanding Officer of the Corps and no deviation permitted. It is expected that scarlet cloth for cuffs, capes and perhaps half facings will be furnished.' (Headquarters, Newburgh, February 24, 1783).

The scarlet cloth arrived from Europe shortly after this and regiments which had not already turned and repaired their coats were ordered to draw lots for the new material. The Light Infantry had already been instructed to wear blue coats faced with white until further orders.

When the War ended the American forces were greatly reduced in number and by mid-June 1783, most of the soldiers had departed for their homes. Only one regular regiment of Infantry was retained and this was dressed in blue coats faced and lined with white.

It will be clear to the reader that never at any time during the conflict did Washington's Army appear as Congress would have wished. Descriptions of uniforms from deserters lists and other official papers are so varied in colours of coats and facings (even among men of the same company) that it is evident that the painter or modeller can make few mistakes, short of blatant anachronisms, in representing the American patriot soldier.

TYPES OF AMERICAN LEATHER HELMETS.
a. Rhode Island Train of Artillery.
b. 2nd South Carolina Infantry Regt.
c. Commander-in-Chief's Guard.

THE COMMANDER-IN-CHIEF'S GUARD

This was a full company of men whose duty it was to protect General Washington, his Staff and headquarters. It consisted of 180 men under the command of an officer ranked as Captain Commandant. The first Guard, formed in March 1776, was disbanded after a plot was discovered among some of its members to assassinate Washington. The Guard was re-formed in 1778 on a more disciplined basis with the stipulation that only native-born Americans were eligible for service. Previously foreigners had been enlisted. Each of the colonies was represented in the new Guard which was composed of men selected from various regiments of the Continental Line at Morristown. The men were at least 5 feet 9 inches in height and their uniforms consisted of blue coats faced and lined buff (after the dress of the Commander-in-Chief) with buff breeches, white crossbelts and stockings and black shoes with brass buckles. The design on the Colours of the Guard show a soldier, presumably a member of the unit, with white facings and blue over white plume in the tricorne but this may be artistic licence or colour fading over the years. The distinguishing mark of the Guard was a scarlet waistcoat, although this is not shown on the figure in the Colours.

At this period the hat was a tricorne edged with white braid but after 1780 a fur crested helmet replaced this. Officers wore boots and the rank distinctions of commissioned ranks of other corps.

TYPES OF AMERICAN LIGHT INFANTRY CAPS.
a. Haslett's Delaware Regiment.
b. 2nd Canadian Regt. (Congress's Own).
c. The later Light Infantry Cap, a pure American design.

LIGHT INFANTRY

Fulfilling the same purpose as Light Company men in the British regiments, the American Light Infantry wore leather caps similar to their opponents. They were first used by the Patriots in 1777 as the companies employed on scouting and skirmishing duties. Washington was so impressed by their mobility and success that he advocated the use of Light troops on a larger scale. The result of his enthusiasm was the banding together of the Light Companies of a number of regiments to form an elite battalion. This battalion was to be used in specialised actions where the skills of Light Infantry would be advantageous. It was so successful that after 1782 it became a permanent feature of the American Army.

By 1779 the Light Infantry, under General Anthony Wayne, numbered almost fourteen hundred men. Apart from their characteristic leather caps, which were worn in a variety of styles, the Light Infantry wore shorter coats than the battalion companies and often wings or shoulder straps in the facing colour or white. Towards the end of the War the facing colour for all Light troops became white. Fusees were carried which were lighter than muskets. Officers wore the Light Infantry cap and the usual rank distinctions.

HUNTING DRESS

As has already been stated, almost every unit of the Patriot Army was obliged, sometime during the War, to dress at least some of their soldiers in hunting dress. More readily associated with riflemen rather than Line troops these hunting shirts and leggings were worn

16

TYPES OF HUNTING SHIRT.
a. Linen with cloth fringe sewn on.
b. Buckskin with cut fringe.

by both and caused their wearers to be known as 'shirtmen'. The style of these clothes varied considerably but all were extremely serviceable and far outlasted the regimental uniform coat. In many cases companies, and even regiments, dyed these shirts a uniform colour and often added collar or cuffs in a facing colour. In this way they were able to maintain the appearance of a uniformed force. The

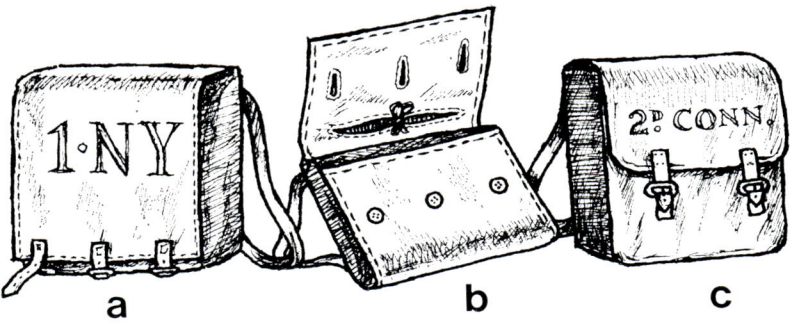

TYPES OF KNAPSACK AND HAVERSACK.
a. Deep flap knapsack of the 1st New York Regt.
b. Home made haversack with flap pocket.
c. Knapsack of the 2nd Connecticut Line.

hunting shirt or 'wamus', as it was called, was either made of tanned buckskin decorated with a cut fringe or of homespun linen, dyed and ornamented with a sewn on coloured fringe. Leggings were similar, often being decorated with Indian beadwork or buckskin thongs. The Indian influence was also seen in the footwear of many of the soldiers, particularly riflemen. Moccasins of laced deerskin were worn and had the soles stuffed with hair or springy moss for comfort. The hunting shirt and leggings were popular with the officers as well as the men. Trumbull's painting of the surrender at Saratoga shows a senior American officer wearing a suit of 'white deerskin' (elkskin tanned to a soft texture like fine white fabric).

INFANTRY EQUIPMENT

The interminable problem of availability of items again dictated the amount of equipment that the foot soldier should carry. Assuming that everything was in order, then an Infantryman's load would consist of a knapsack (perhaps with a blanket roll on top), a haversack, a cartridge box, a canteen or water bottle and either a bayonet and musket or a rifle. Knapsacks were made by the Americans in a variety of styles, often in their own homes. Size also varied considerably and many captured examples were in use. The home-made ones were usually oil-cloth, linen or duck and were often weather-proofed in red ochre paint, sometimes having the initials or cypher of the regiment painted across the flap. The blanket roll, when carried, could be either rolled and strapped across the top of the knapsack, or wrapped around the body over the left shoulder and tied at the right hip.

Haversacks were even more varied in style and size than the knapsacks and many hunting bags or Indian pouches served this purpose. The most common type of water container was the round wooden canteen made up of a number of staves held in place by oak hoops and waterproofed by painting or by covering with prepared linen. It had a carved stopper made of wood or bone which was attached to the carrying strap by a thong. Some men painted 'U. STATES' or the initials or names of their regiments on the canteens. Other types of water bottle made of tinned

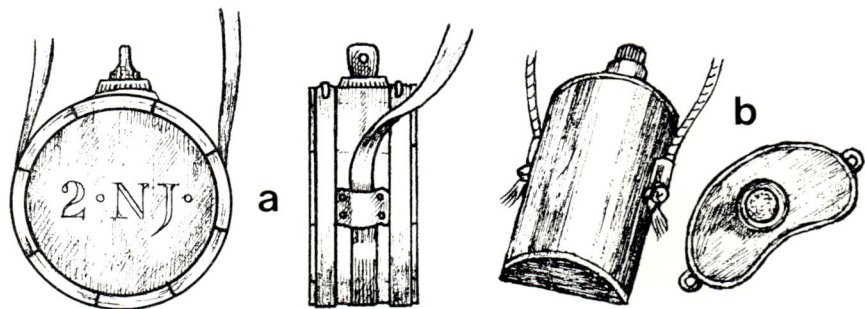

TYPES OF WATER BOTTLE.
a. Front and side views of the popular wooden canteen.
b. Two shapes of the tin sheet type of flask.

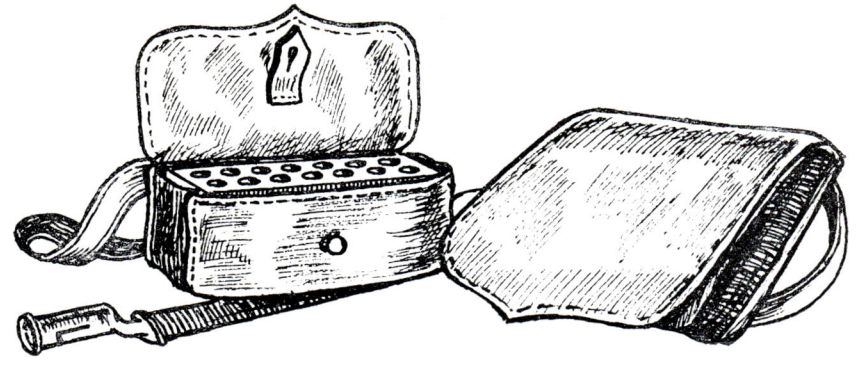

BAYONET AND CARTRIDGE POUCHES. Many pouches were home made and varied considerably in style and size.

iron sheet were widely used and often a metal drinking cup would be attached to the canteens. Cartridge boxes were carried on a shoulder belt and were usually worn over the right hip. They consisted of a leather bag often fitted with a wooden former which was drilled with holes to carry something like two dozen cartridges. These paper cartridges were made up of a lead ball resting on sufficient black powder to prime and charge the weapon. As an alternative to the shoulder pouch, cartridges were often carried in a smaller box worn on the front of the body on a waist belt. If the musket balls were carried loose in a pouch, then a powder horn was worn hanging from a leather shoulder strap. The horns were frequently scraped thin so that the amount of powder being used could be checked by holding the horn up to the light. They were often decorated with carvings of animals, birds, maps and the like.

Bayonets were suspended from either shoulder or waist belts and were carried in leather scabbards with metal fittings. Some bayonet belts also had provision for a sword or hanger to be carried. Muskets and rifles are dealt with in the section of the book dealing with weapons. It was not uncommon for soldiers to carry an Indian knife or tomahawk, particularly the riflemen and those men experienced in Indian fighting. The following instruction was issued in Massachusetts in April 1779 and gives a good impression of how the revolutionary soldier was expected to equip:

'You are hereby ordered and directed, to compleat yourself with ARMS and Accoutrements, by the 12th Instant, upon failure thereof, you are liable to a FINE of THREE POUNDS: and for every Sixty Days after, a FINE of SIX POUNDS, agreable to Law.

Articles of Equipment

A good Fire-Arm, with a Steel or Iron Ram-Rod, and a Spring to retain the same, a Worm, Priming wire and Brush, and a Bayonet fitted to your GUN, a Scabbard and Belt therefor, and a Cutting Sword, or a Tomahawk or Hatchet, a Pouch containing a Cartridge Box, that will hold fifteen Rounds of Cartridges at least, a hundred Buck-Shot, a Jack-Knife and Tow for Wadding, six Flints, one pound

POWDER HORN AND TYPES OF TOMAHAWK.
The horn is inscribed with a typical motto.
One of the trade tomahawks has a head incorporating a pipe bowl.

Powder, forty Leaden Balls fitted to your GUN, a Knapsack and Blanket, a Canteen or Wooden Bottle sufficient to hold one Quart.'

INFANTRY WEAPONS

Shoulder Weapons: Muskets used by the Patriots included the British Brown Bess and French Charleville models left over from the French and Indian Wars. Both of these weapons provided patterns for the Americans to produce their own muskets. These were organised by the Committees of Safety, bodies set up in each of the colonies with the responsibility of providing arms for the Patriots. This American version of the Brown Bess musket which was used by so many of the Continental Line was, later in the War, gradually replaced by new Charlevilles brought over by Washington's French allies.

The other principal shoulder-arm of the Revolution was the rifle. Of the many styles of rifle in use the most famous was the Kentucky. This, in fact, is a misnomer as the weapon was developed by German gunsmiths of Lancaster County, Pennsylvania. The 'Kentucky' probably originated from the fact that these rifles were used in great numbers throughout the wilderness southwest of Pennsylvania which was Kentucky. The calibres of the rifles were anything between ·30 and ·80. The octagonal barrel was rifled with seven grooves which turned the ball approximately once from breech to muzzle. Characteristic of the weapon was the patch box cut into the right side of the stock and fitted with a hinged lid. This box varied in size from weapon to weapon. Prior to the Revolution these Kentucky flintlocks were made with flat-ended butts but these were later changed to a crescent shape. The rifle fired a lighter ball than the musket and had a greater range and accuracy. It was primarily used in sharpshooting tactics by marksmen selecting individual targets, rather than for volley firing. These marksmen often fought among ranks of musketmen giving covering fire as the soldiers reloaded. Washington disapproved of riflemen operating alone

20

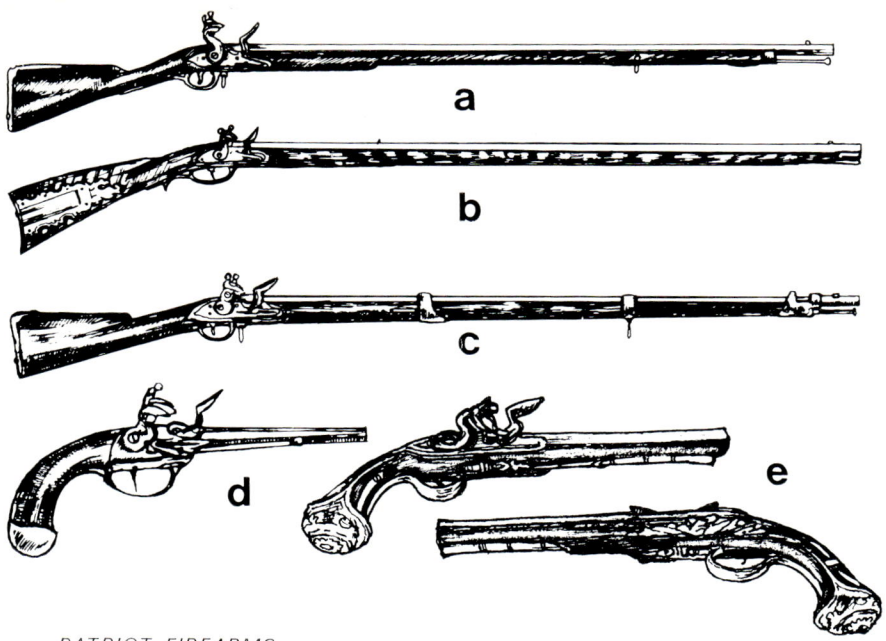

PATRIOT FIREARMS.
a. American Committee of Safety Musket.
b. Type of Kentucky Rifle.
c. French Charleville Musket.
d. French Charleville Pistol, Model 1777, ·69 calibre.
e. Flintlocks belonging to General Washington.

because of the disadvantages of the weapon. It had a slow loading rate (a well trained musketman could fire three rounds to a rifleman's one) and did not have facilities for attaching a bayonet. This last point prompted Washington to instruct that all riflemen should carry folding spears as a bayonet substitute. These were to be carried across the back on a leather sling. Over the years legends have grown around the uncanny marksmanship of the American rifleman but there is no doubt that, despite the part played by the rifle during the Revolution, it was the musket that carried the firepower and won the battles.

Pistols: Early in the War, when the Committees of Safety commissioned private gunsmiths to produce weapons for the Patriots, priority was naturally given to shoulder arms over handguns. Pistols certainly were made by these American smiths but only one record remains of a specified pattern. This is the Rappahannock Forge pistol, a gun of about 15 inches overall length, having a 9 inch, ·69 calibre smooth bore barrel and a heavy butt of a hexagonal shape. It is supposed that only about one hundred or so of these pistols were manufactured. The majority of handguns used during the War were of British, Scottish or French origin. It is also known that weapons were purchased from Prussia. Pistols were carried principally by officers, especially in the Navy, where it was found that the pistol and blunderbuss were parti-

21

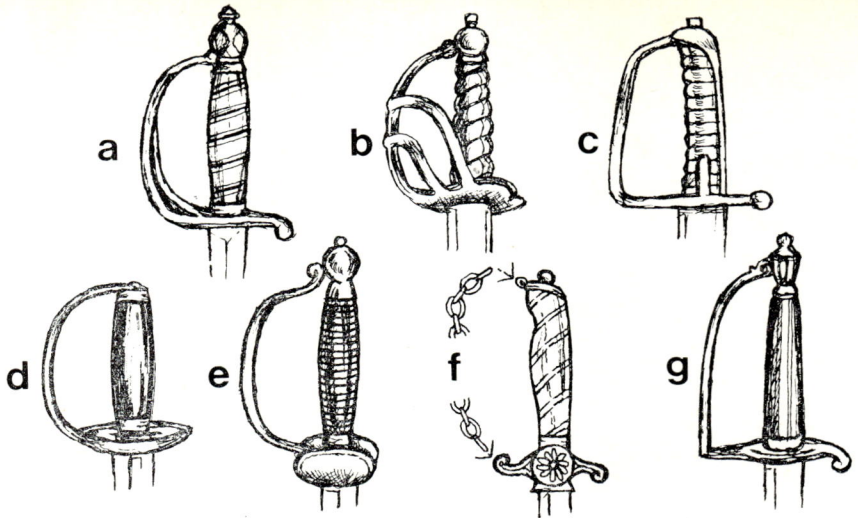

INFANTRY SWORDS.

a. and b. are typical of the heavier type of Infantry officers sword.

c. French model hanger with brass hilt.
   (30 in. overall length).

d. Popular style of Infantry sword. Four of this type have been
   excavated. (Double edged 31 in. overall length).

e. Type of small sword favoured by many officers.

f. Bone handled hunting sword of the type worn by some senior
   officers (Washington and Steuben had them). Not a combat weapon.
   32 in. overall length.

g. Another popular model. A Spadroon.

cularly suited to boarding party tactics (all blunderbusses were ordered
to be turned over to the fleet in August, 1776). As a supplementary
measure, Congress set up repair depots throughout the colonies to
maintain the constant stream of damaged weapons. As with all other
equipment used by the Patriots, a great number of pistols were captured
British or Hessian types.

Swords: Patriots enlisting in the Army often brought along their own
edge weapons, either a family sword or a home-made one. A number of
specimens of one particular type of sword have been found. The style
suggests that local blacksmiths produced these weapons to a basic
pattern. At the beginning of the Revolution an allowance was given to
soldiers bringing their own swords to the Army but later on central
storehouses were set up and troops were supplied from stocks manufactured by private swordsmiths under contract. Many British and
French swords were also much in evidence.

French Grenadier swords of the 1767 pattern were issued to some
Continental Line troops. There exist examples of these with blades
marked 'Grenadier of Virginia'. Often only the blades were imported
and the hilts were fitted in the colonies.

Bayonets were scarce throughout the Army and many soldiers of the
Line were without them.

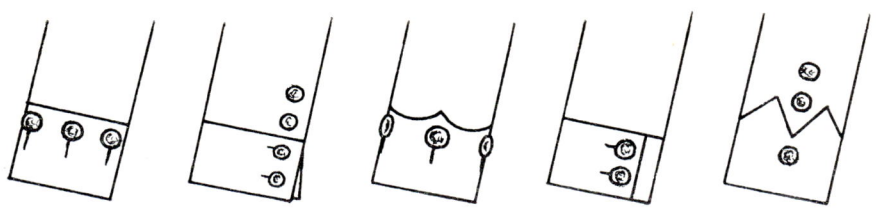

OFFICER'S CUFF STYLES (From contemporary portraits).

OFFICERS

Congress was responsible for the appointment of senior officers. When Washington became Commander-in-Chief in 1775, he had Artemas Ward, Charles Lee, Philip Schuyler and Israel Putnam as his Major-Generals. Commissions of Colonel and below were decreed by the colonies and this resulted in the American officer corps being something of a mixed bag. Some had field experience, having served in the British Army during the French and Indian Wars but a great number were only Militia officers elected in their own areas on a popularity basis rather than a military one. If a man could drum up enough neighbours to form a company he became a captain; should he find sufficient for a regiment he could be a colonel. Washington adopted a strong line over commissions and saw to it that several unsuitable militia officers were cashiered.

Many officers of the Militia did, however, make fine Continental commanders and some, such as Nathaniel Greene of Rhode Island, became Generals. It is well known that Washington preferred his Continental officers to be gentlemen and this attracted the best of the young men from the plantation and merchant families of the colonies. Adapting themselves to the necessity of learning quickly in war and inspired by the example of their Commander-in-Chief a great number of these officers became more than a match for their British counterparts.

Officers' Dress: Rank distinctions for officers were the same in all arms of the Patriot forces, so that although this section is devoted specifically to Infantry, rank badges would be the same in the Cavalry, Artillery or Engineers.

General Orders of July 1775 directed that General Officers and their Aides were to be distinguished by the wearing of broad coloured ribands across the body from the right shoulder to the left hip, worn over the waistcoat and under the regimental coat. Officers of Field rank and below were to adopt a system of hat cockades or plumes of various colours. The distinctions were as follows:

The Commander-in-Chief to wear a light blue riband; Major-Generals and Brigadier Generals a pink riband (Major-Generals were shortly after changed to a purple riband); Aides and Majors of Brigade, a green riband; Colonels, Lt. Colonels and Majors a red or pink cockade in the hat; Captains a yellow or buff cockade; Subalterns a green cockade.

STYLES OF WEARING THE REGIMENTAL COAT.
a. The buttoned over lapel favoured by many officers.
b. The lapels buttoned back, although not all
   the buttons are fastened.

Apart from these distinctions there would be little to distinguish an officer from his men. When in uniform he would wear basically the same style of regimental coat as a private, although usually of finer material and cut. The lapels of the coat were frequently worn fastened across the body in double-breasted fashion. Gorgets might be seen on some officers but these were usually relics of previous service in the French and Indian Wars. Officers on duty did at times wear waist sashes and carry spontoons but there was little ruling about this.

Headgear was as varied among the commissioned ranks as it was among the men. The official cap was the cocked hat but even these were worn in a variety of styles. Knee length breeches of linen, buckskin or wool broadcloth were worn with cotton or woollen stockings which were produced in many different colours. Waistcoats were of fine wool or linen and were usually single-breasted with flapped pockets. Footwear consisted of spatterdashes and shoes, or boots styled to the liking of the wearer. Linen overalls or hunting leggings were also popular. Swords and bayonets were worn on waist or shoulder belts

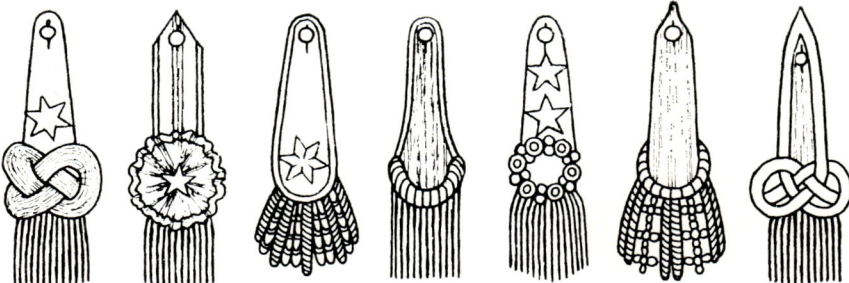

TYPES OF OFFICER'S EPAULETTES.
There was little uniformity in epaulette design,
particularly among senior officers.

STYLES OF OFFICER'S COCKED HATS.
(From contemporary pictures). Note the
wide variety of cockades.

and most officers carried muskets or fusils and sometimes pistols. Again, it was largely a question of personal preference and availability of weapons.

Congress resolved on November 25, 1779, 'that the following articles be delivered as a suit of clothes for the current and every succeeding year of their service to the Officers of the Line and Staff, entitled by any resolution of Congress to receive the same, viz: one hat, one watch-coat, one body-coat, four vests (one for winter, three for summer), four pairs of breeches (two for winter and two for summer), four shirts, six pairs of stockings (three pair thereof worsted and three of thread), four pairs of shoes.'

A General Order issued in June of the following year stated that, 'all Officers, as well Warrant as commissioned, to wear a cockade

At the Battle of Monmouth on June 28, 1778, as a result of General Lee's mismanagement and his lack of communication with Washington, the American troops retreated from the field. When Washington heard of the fiasco he hastened to Lee and rebuked him, afterwards taking command of the Patriots and leading them to victory. This print gives a good comparison between the more official dress of senior officers and the utility dress of the foot soldier. Washington is on the right.

and side-arms, either a sword or a genteel bayonet'. The same order specified a new system of rank markings for officers as follows:

'Major-Generals to wear a blue coat with buff facings, yellow buttons, white or buff underclothes (waistcoat and breeches), two epaulettes with two stars on each and a black and white feather in the hat. (White below, black above). Brigadier-Generals—As above but with one star on each epaulette and a white hat feather. Colonels, Lieut. Colonels and Majors to wear Regimental uniforms with two epaulettes. Captains to wear Regimental uniform with one epaulette on the right shoulder. Subalterns to wear Regimental uniform with one epaulette on the left shoulder. (All officers' epaulettes were gold). Aides-de-Camp to wear uniform of their rank and Corps, or, if they belong to no Corps, of their General Officers. Aides of Major Generals and Brigadier Generals to have green hat feathers, those of the Commander-in-Chief a white and green feather. The Adjutant General and his Aide to wear the uniform of their own Corps and a green over red feather. Sub and Brigade Inspectors to wear the uniform of their rank and a blue hat feather. Such of the staff as have military rank to wear the uniforms of their ranks of the Corps to which they belong in the Line. Such as have no military rank to wear plain coats with a cockade and sword.'

When it appeared that the entry of France into the War was imminent, Washington wrote, 'It is recommended to the Officers to have black and white cockades, a black ground with a white relief—emblamation of the expected union of the two armies.' The colours of the cockade were sometimes reversed; a portrait of Alexander Hamilton in Light Infantry cap shows black on a white ground.

This then was how Washington's officers should have appeared between 1775 and 1783. Needless to say few of them did. Badges of rank make inviting targets for enemy marksmen and in any case the very nature of the War, with clothing and refinements in short supply, would oblige officers, especially those below field rank, to patch and repair their coats as the men had to. Hunting dress was, of course, as popular with commissioned ranks as it was with the men.

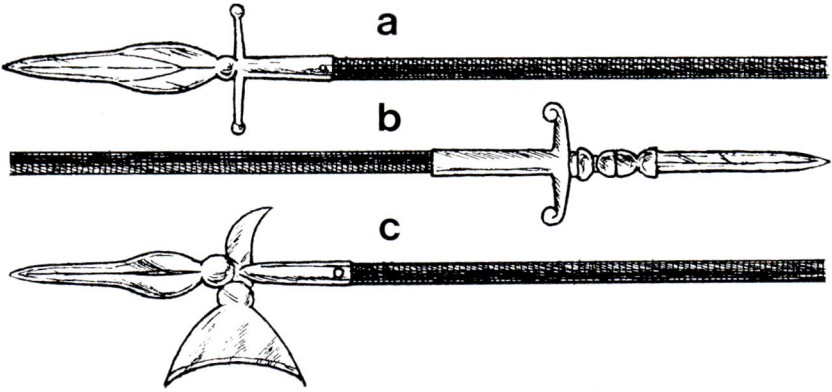

AMERICAN POLE WEAPONS.
a. and b. are types of Officer's Spontoon.
c. Type of Sergeant's Halberd.

NON COMMISSIONED OFFICERS

The Order of July 23, 1775 establishing rank distinctions for officers also made provision for sergeants and corporals. Sergeants were to be distinguished by an epaulette or stripe of red cloth worn on the right shoulder; corporals were to wear one of green. The Order of June 18, 1780, which directed officers to wear 'a sword or genteel bayonet', also applied to warrant officers. In parade dress sergeants would have carried a halberd.

Towards the end of the War, rank distinctions for NCOs were changed. General Orders from Newburgh on May 14, 1782 stated that, 'The clothier is, if possible, to obtain worsted shoulder knots for the NCOs. The Sergeants are to be distinguished by one on each shoulder and the Corporals by one on the right shoulder; and in the meantime it is proposed that a piece of white cloth should be substituted by way of distinction.'

FIFE CASE. A cord through the eyelets on the sides prevented the lid from becoming detached when open. This case bears the crest of the 2nd. Canadian Regt. (Congress's Own).

MUSICIANS

Musicians of the Infantry fell into two categories, drummers and fifers. Drummers were the more important of the two, being employed not only in producing music on the march, but also in beating the many drum calls so essential in an eighteenth century army. Von Steuben's regulations give these routine drum calls and their purposes:

'The different daily beats shall begin on the right, and be instantly followed by the whole army; to facilitate which, the drummer's call shall be beat by the drums of the police, a quarter of an hour before beating, when the drummers will assemble before the colours of their respective battalions. The General is to beat only when the whole are to march, and is the signal to strike the tents, and prepare for the march. The Assembly is the signal to repair to the colours. The March for the whole to move. The Reveillie is beat at day-break, and is the signal for the soldiers to rise, and the sentries to leave off challenging. The Troop assembles the soldiers together, for the purpose of calling and roll inspecting the men for duty. The Retreat is beat at sun-set, for the calling of the roll, warning the men for duty, and reading the orders of the day. The Tattoo is for the soldiers to repair to their tents, where they must remain till reveillie beating next morning.' (There seems to have been no Taps.) 'To Arms, is a signal for getting under arms in case of an alarm. The Parley is to desire a conference with the enemy.'

The Patriots followed the British practice of reversing the coat colours for musicians (ie, the body of the coat was made in the facing colour and the collar, cuffs and lapels were in the coat colour). Paintings of musicians by contemporary artists show considerable variations in other distinctions. In some cases worsted epaulettes or shoulder wings are shown in the lapel colour and in one instance a drummer is shown having the pocket flaps of the coat in the colour of the lapel. It is probable that the Colonel would decide how his regiment's musicians should appear, keeping in mind the availability of cloth. Some painters have depicted musicians in regular regimental coats without the colours

This print of the embarkation of Montgomery's troops at Crown Point shows the somewhat civilian appearance of the Patriots in the early part of the Revolution. Many variations may be seen in leg-wear, cuffs, turnbacks, etc. The drummer on the right shows how the drum was carried on the march. The men appear to be marching in columns of four.

reversed and no doubt many did appear this way. Hats were like those of the rank and file. In the later stages of the War a leather cap with front plate, like those of the Light Infantry, was prescribed for musicians but it is doubtful if this was ever worn by more than a few bandsmen. Musicians also wore a hanger, when available, usually carried in a frog on a buff waist belt. Drums had the hoops painted in red or sometimes the facing colour of the regiment and often the shell was decorated with a motif, either regimental or of a patriotic nature. In April, 1775 the Patriots adopted the motto 'QUI TRANSTULIT SUSTINET' for use on their flags and drums. Drums were carried in the usual manner on a shoulder belt usually fitted with loops to hold the drumsticks. Fifes were carried in cylindrical cases about 15 inches in length, made of painted metal or wood and slung on a shoulder cord. As with the drums many had motifs painted upon them.

SPECIAL DISTINCTIONS

Long Service Stripes: Later in the War long service markings were specified for the Continental Army. An Order of June 17, 1782 reads:

'NCOs and Privates who have served four years in any Continental Regiment, shall be entitled to wear one stripe of white tape on the left sleeve of the Regimental coat, which shall extend from seam to seam, upper part of the sleeve three inches from and parallel from the shoulder seam so that the tape may form a herring bone figure. Eight years service, a second stripe set one inch below the first.'

On August 11, 1782 an amendment to this Order specified long service stripes to be in the facing colour of the regiment and not always in white as previously stipulated. Holders of long service stripes found guilty of misconduct might lose these distinctions, being divested of them at a public ceremony.

Good Conduct Stripes:

'More than three years clean record, a narrow piece of white cloth of an angular form, fixed to the left arm of the Regimental coat. More than six years to be distinguished by two pieces of cloth set on parallel to each other in a similar form.'

These markings could also be forfeited for misconduct.

The Purple Heart: The Purple Heart, now awarded in the American forces for a wound sustained on active service, was introduced during the Revolution. At this time it was presented for 'Any single meritorious action . . . the author of it shall be entitled to wear on his facings, over the left breast, the figure of a heart in purple cloth or silk edged with narrow lace or binding'. (HQ Newburgh, August 7, 1782).

3: Infantry of the Thirteen Colonies

OF the numerous regiments which served the Patriot cause relatively few exact uniform details remain. The following is an analysis of some of the more tangible evidence.

NEW HAMPSHIRE REGIMENTS

2nd NEW HAMPSHIRE REGIMENT (CONTINENTAL LINE). Enoch Poor was the Regiment's Colonel when it was raised in May, 1775. The following year the regiment was assigned to the Second Brigade and in 1777 with its new commanding officer, Colonel Hale, was taken prisoner almost to a man. At this time the uniform of the 2nd New Hampshire Regiment was a sky blue coat with red facings and white linings, buckskin breeches and waistcoats and buff cross belts. The pewter buttons were stamped with the state name and regimental number and the tricorne had no edging tape. This colour uniform was specified for Captain Caleb Robinson's Company but it is extremely likely that the other companies were dressed the same.

The re-organisation of 1779 ordered blue coats faced white for New Hampshire troops and as a supply of clothing was forthcoming from France at about this time it is possible that some regiments from the state may have acquired white facings.

The 2nd New Hampshire had two Colours; one light blue grey and one buff. Both were captured by the British a short while before Saratoga.

A number of New Hampshire men were in the early formation of the Green Mountain Rangers under Colonel Ethan Allen raised in 1771, but at this time there were no official uniforms and buckskins were the usual dress. The re-organised Green Mountain Boys are dealt with among the New York regiments.

MASSACHUSETTS REGIMENTS

The dress of the Massachusetts men who fought at Lexington and Bunker Hill has already been described. After these actions regiments from the colony, in the Continental service, were dressed in a variety of coat colours. Independent Cadet or Bodyguard Companies were usually dressed in red coats with various coloured facings. Short brown coats were common. The proceedings of the Massachusetts Provincial Congress of July, 1775 specify coats without any lapels although it is known that both red and white facings were common. Throughout the entire War, however, it is most likely that blue coats faced white were worn by the majority of Massachusetts soldiers.

Newspaper reports of May, 1776, list Captain Gilbert Speakman's Company of the **14th CONTINENTAL REGIMENT** (raised in Massachusetts) as being dressed in light coloured coats with red lapels, buckskin breeches and blue stockings. Also white cap, frock and trousers and blue coats with leather buttons and tarred trousers are mentioned.

THE 14th MASSACHUSETTS REGIMENT (not to be confused with the 14th Continental) were reputed to have worn brown coats faced light blue.

THE 2nd MASSACHUSETTS REGIMENT was formed out of the 23rd Continental Regiment of 1776. Their coats were blue faced white and lined white (sometimes red) Waistcoats often had sleeves and were of wool or linen coloured white, green or brown. Overalls replaced breeches after 1776. (White for summer wear and blue or brown for winter). Buckskin leggings were also frequently worn.

The men of Colonel Asa Whitcomb's **6th CONTINENTALS (MASSACHUSETTS)** known as Whitcomb's Rangers wore blue or blue faced white coats. This regiment wintered in early 1777 around the shore of Lake Champlain and as a result many of the men adopted seamen's clothing.

Washington's specifications of 1779 were, for all Massachusetts regiments, blue coats with white facings.

RHODE ISLAND REGIMENTS

Raised in May, 1775 **THE 2nd RHODE ISLAND REGIMENT** was originally called the 2nd Regiment of the Army of Observation of Rhode Island. This was a brigade consisting of three Infantry regiments and an Artillery train. In 1775 the regiment was numbered the 14th Foot and in the re-organisation of the following January became the 11th Continental Infantry. In 1777, under Colonel Israel Angell, it was titled the 2nd Rhode Island Regiment of the Rhode Island Line. Almost a year to the day after this, the 1st and 2nd Rhode Island Regiments were amalgamated under Colonel Jeremiah Olney for the remainder of the War.

The Rhode Island Train of Artillery wore brown coats and, as the 2nd Regiment of Infantry was also clothed by the Colony, it is likely that during the early part of the Revolution they too were dressed in brown probably with red or white facings. Later, officers are reported to have furnished their own coats cut to their own styling and in blue faced with red.

After 1779, the regiment seems to have been well equipped with some of the men in linen rifle shirts and overalls, and others in white coats or jackets. Hats were edged with white lace.

Officially, blue coats with white facings were the colours chosen for Rhode Island Regiments in 1779.

CONNECTICUT REGIMENTS

At the outbreak of the Revolution, the Connecticut companies reporting for duty were clothed mostly in red. These red coats were soon changed to brown however, with the exception of the **GOVERNOR'S FOOTGUARDS**. The first company of this unit had black facings and the second company buff facings. Eventually this uniform, which, having a bearskin cap, was dangerously similar to the dress of the British Grenadier Companies was abandoned in favour of more serviceable garb.

Many of the **4th CONNECTICUT REGIMENT** at Valley Forge were clothed in short double-breasted coats without lapels but having a red collar and pointed red cuffs. A great variety of leg wear seems to have been worn including brown cloth or buckskin breeches, linen overalls or rifle leggings.

THE 14th CONNECTICUT REGIMENT wore brown coats faced red with the buttons (and perhaps the officer's shoulder belt plates) engraved with the numerals, 14.

THE 2nd CONNECTICUT REGIMENT is said to have worn brown coats with white facings.

Despite the 1779 ruling that Connecticut regiments were to have dark blue coats faced white, most of the colony's troops seem to have served throughout the War in some type of brown uniform with buff, white or red facings or with no facings at all.

NEW YORK REGIMENTS

Early in 1775, New York Province raised four regiments for Continental service. All four served with General Montgomery through his Quebec campaign. Each of the regiments was dressed in different coloured coats.

THE 1st REGIMENT (Colonel Alexander McDougall's) wore blue coats faced and lined red. It served in many major engagements including Trenton, Saratoga and Yorktown. Red facings were worn until 1779 when all New York troops were instructed to wear buff facings. Red was again adopted, however, when buff cloth became scarce in 1782.

THE 2nd REGIMENT (Colonel Goose von Schaick's) wore light brown coats faced blue.

THE 3rd REGIMENT (Colonel James Clinton's) was also known as the Ulster Regiment or 3rd Yorkers and was dressed in brown coats faced green and lined white. The men were particularly well equipped.

THE 4th REGIMENT (Colonel James Holme's) was clothed in dark brown coats with scarlet facings.

All four of the New York regiments wore the rifle shirt on many occasions. As coats wore out they were replaced with hunting dress until new uniforms were available. Late in the War these regiments are said to have received buckskin waistcoats and woollen breeches, mittens and caps.

All New York regiments were scheduled for blue coats faced buff in 1779.

The raising of a new regiment of **GREEN MOUNTAIN RANGERS** was authorised by Continental and New York Congresses in July, 1775. Colonel Seth Warner was in command of the five hundred men who served under Montgomery and Schuyler up to the advance on Quebec. They wore green coats with green turnbacks and lapels and only the collar and cuffs faced red, black cocked hats, buckskin breeches and waistcoats and woollen stockings. Many had checked shirts. Rifle shirts were often worn over or instead of uniform coats. Not all the men were furnished with bayonets. A portrait of Lieutenant Ira Allen of this regiment shows an officer's parade dress of black hat laced gold, gold epaulette on a green coat with scarlet facings and white turnbacks, crimson sash and buff waistcoat and breeches. Officers carried fusees or muskets on duty.

NEW JERSEY REGIMENTS

The men raised by New Jersey for service with the Continental Line were mostly clothed in blue coats faced red. The **3rd NEW JERSEY REGIMENT** (Colonel Elias Dayton's) was named the Jersey Blues and was dressed in regimental coats of blue faced red with white linings. The pewter buttons were stamped with the name of the colony and the regimental number. Although this was the official uniform there was much variation throughout the regiment. All colours of small clothes (waistcoat and breeches) were worn but mainly blue and white. Some were buckskin and others cloth. Both leather caps and tricornes were to be seen and the women of Newwark, New Jersey, made for some of the men working dress of dyed blue cloth.

The dress regulations of 1779 instructed New Jersey Regiments to wear blue coats faced buff and white smallclothes.

PENNSYLVANIA REGIMENTS

THE 1st PENNSYLVANIA BATTALION commanded by Colonel John Bull from November 1775 to January 1776 was the basis for the formation of the 2nd Pennsylvania Regiment of the Pennsylvania Line of the Continental Army formed in October 1776. The uniform was a brown coat with buff facings and pewter buttons stamped with the Regimental number. Waistcoats were white and breeches buff. Some of the companies of the Battalion were dressed differently to this in brown coats faced green, or blue coats faced white; in fact in whatever clothing was available.

In 1779 the colours for Pennsylvania Regiments were blue coats faced red and many were able to obtain these uniforms. On parade, sergeants of this regiment held their muskets at the advance when the men were at shoulder or support. In the latter part of the War the Sergeants, as well as making the regulation change from one red epaulette to two white knots, wore a red worsted sash and carried a short sabre. Some men of this regiment were detached for service as marines on American vessels.

The 1st REGIMENT OF CONTINENTAL LINE (1776) was formed

from Thompson's Pennsylvania Rifles of June 1775 and became in January 1777 the 1st Pennsylvania Regiment of the Pennsylvania Line (Colonel Edward Hands) and was dressed in brown coats faced green or, on campaign, in rifle shirts and leggings.

THE **PENNSYLVANIA STATE REGIMENT** was raised in April 1777 and the regiment was transferred to the Continental Service. It was officially designated the 13th Pennsylvania Regiment in November 1777. The uniform was a blue coat faced and lined red with pewter buttons stamped 'P.R.S'.

THE **6th PENNSYLVANIA BATTALION** of the Continental Line wore blue coats faced and lined red with buff smallclothes. Other Pennsylvania regiments and their recorded colours are as follows:

Unit	Colours
3rd PENNSYLVANIA BATTALION	Brown faced white
4th PENNSYLVANIA RIFLE REGIMENT	Brown faced white
5th PENNSYLVANIA LINE	Blue faced white
6th PENNSYLVANIA LINE	Blue faced red
7th PENNSYLVANIA LINE	Blue faced white
9th PENNSYLVANIA LINE	Brown faced red
10th PENNSYLVANIA LINE	Blue faced red
OLD 11th PENNSYLVANIA LINE	Some blue faced red; others green faced white
LATER 11th PENNSYLVANIA LINE	Blue faced red

It must be realised, of course, that there were always variations and discrepancies in the dress of these units.

Officially, after 1779, Pennsylvania Regiments should have worn blue coats faced red.

DELAWARE REGIMENTS

Delaware contributed one of the best equipped crack units of the War in **HASLETT'S DELAWARE REGIMENT**. The uniform was a blue coat, shorter than usual, with red facings and linings. Waistcoat, breeches and stockings were white and black spatterdashes were worn as well as white or buff crossbelts. Caps of Light Company style in jacked leather were worn by the whole regiment. The front of the cap carried gilt painted motifs declaring 'LIBERTY AND INDEPENDENCE' around a wheatsheaf surmounted by a ship and with the inscription, 'DELAWARE REGIMENT' on a lower scroll. On parade all ranks wore a red plume on the left of the cap rising from the cockade.

Delaware Regiments were to have blue coats faced red by Washington's order of 1779.

MARYLAND REGIMENTS

Maryland authorised the raising of seven independent companies in January, 1776. These companies campaigned together as one large battalion under a single field officer, Major Mordecai Gist. The Company saw service as part of the Continental Army around New York. **THE 4th INDEPENDENT COMPANY OF MARYLAND STATE TROOPS** was part of this battalion and had James Hindman as its Captain. The dress of the company consisted of linen hunting shirts dyed purple with red collars and cuffs, buckskin breeches and black spatterdashes and cocked hats laced white. They were armed with muskets. Late in 1776 the company was disbanded and the men joined other Maryland forces.

SMALLWOOD'S MARYLAND REGIMENT was another of the crack regiments of the Patriot Army and fought alongside the above battalion. The regiment had the not too common distinction of being dressed in red coats with buff facings and linings. Buttons were pewter and waistcoats and breeches were generally buff. The cocked hat was laced white.

THE 2nd MARYLAND REGIMENT raised in December 1776 was uniformed for the most part in blue coats faced red. These were the colours specified in 1779 for all Maryland troops although the scarcity of cloth would make the wearing of hunting clothes inevitable.

VIRGINIA REGIMENTS

Little is on record regarding the uniform of the Infantry of Virginia. Before the Revolution the Virginia Militia, Washington's own regiment, wore blue coats faced red, and as some of the Virginia Light Horse wore these colours in 1776 it seems reasonable to suppose that other regiments may have been clothed in similar uniforms. Virginian Rangers and other irregulars had fought against Pontiac's Indians in 1763 in hunting dress and continued to wear this costume during the Revolution.

All Virginia regiments were instructed to wear blue coats faced red with white linings in the re-organisation of 1779.

NORTH CAROLINA REGIMENTS

The province of North Carolina raised ten regiments of Infantry for Continental service between 1775 and 1782. **THE 3rd NORTH CAROLINA REGIMENT** is reputed to have worn hunting or rifle shirts of buckskin with woollen overalls in winter and linen in summer. Hats were reputedly, 'turned up round hats'. Equipment was assorted, being either American made or captured. Officers also wore this dress.

The North Carolina regiments were instructed to wear blue coats faced lighter blue and lined white with the buttonholes bound in white tape. The complexity of this uniform would suggest that if any were worn at all they would have been restricted to some officers or at the most to a few companies.

SOUTH CAROLINA REGIMENTS

THE 1st SOUTH CAROLINA REGIMENT OF INFANTRY was raised in June 1775, initially to defend the colony, but soon being sent on Continental service. Uniforms consisted of blue jackets faced red with white linings. Unlike the standard pattern of regimental coat this regiment is usually shown wearing short jackets without tails. Waistcoats and breeches were worn, with black spatterdashes in full dress and linen overalls on service. The headgear of the regiment was unusual being a black leather peaked cap with a white thread tassel on top and a white metal crescent on the front bearing the legend, 'ULTIMA-RATIO'.

THE 2nd SOUTH CAROLINA REGIMENT OF INFANTRY was dressed in a similar uniform, but the crescents on the caps were engraved, 'LIBERTY OR DEATH' or perhaps just, 'LIBERTY'. An old engraving of this regiment shows the leather caps to have a fur tail or plumes across the top and coats to be short double-breasted jackets.

Both regiments were extremely well equipped and possessed two Colours each, one of blue and one of red embroidered silk. Their most famous action was in the defence of Fort Moultrie on Sullivan's Island.

The 1779 Regulations specified blue coats faced lighter blue with white linings and button hole tape for all the regiments of South Carolina.

GEORGIA REGIMENTS

The dress of Georgia Regiments is not well documented and the costume worn by THE 1st GEORGIA REGIMENT OF THE CONTINENTAL LINE was probably typical of that worn throughout the state. It is unlikely that the regiment possessed any uniforms before the re-organisation of 1779. Some of the officers are reputed to have worn blue coats faced red for full dress, but in the field they would wear the hunting dress adopted by the men. At first leather breeches were worn with the rifle shirt but after 1777 overalls of wool for winter and linen for summer replaced these. Cocked hats had no edging lace and most of the other equipment was captured material.

After 1779 Georgia regiments were instructed to wear blue coats faced lighter blue with white linings and buttonhole tape but it is unlikely that they ever did.

OTHER REGIMENTS

These other regiments were units on Continental service which have not been included under colonial headings because they were recruited on a wider basis than a single province.

SHERBURNE'S CONTINENTAL REGIMENT was one of the sixteen Continental Infantry Regiments authorised by Congress in December, 1776. The sixteen regiments were not numbered but were called by the names of their colonels. Most of the men came from Connecticut but many were recruited elsewhere. In 1779 they appear to have been well equipped in a most distinctive uniform consisting of a brown coat faced yellow and lined white. Waistcoats and breeches were dark green and white stockings with black spatterdashes were worn. Knapsacks and haversacks were of painted canvas and crossbelts were white leather. The cocked hats were edged in white wool braid.

Some of the other fifteen additional regiments organised with Sherburne's were Forman's, Gist's, Grayson's, Hartley's, Henley's, Jackson's, Lee's, Patton's (called Foot Guards), Spencer's (called Foot Guards), Warner's, Webb's and the German Battalion (Haussegger's).

2nd CANADIAN REGIMENT (CONGRESS'S OWN) was raised during 1776 and was composed of men from all the colonies and Canada (although most came from Pennsylvania and Canada). It gained a reputation as an excellent corps throughout the War. Up to 1779 the uniform was a brown coat with white facings and linings. After this date the facings were changed to red. Waistcoats and breeches were white. Battalion companies wore white braided cocked hats but the most popular image of the regiment is created by the Light Company who wore low black caps made of six pieces of jacked leather with an upright leather panel in front painted with the interwoven letters 'C.O.R.' and the motto, 'PRO ARIS ET FOCIS' on a scroll. Some of the equipment worn was captured from the British.

4: Cavalry

WASHINGTON was primarily an Infantry general and gave little thought to Cavalry as a striking force. This resulted in the horse troops always being employed in a secondary role to that of the foot soldiers and Artillery. Until 1776 there was no organised Cavalry. In July of that year Connecticut sent four hundred Light Horse to Washington in New York. The men were mainly from the higher social classes and, whilst they were prepared to serve in a cavalier role, refused to involve themselves in the mundane duties of camp life such as performing guard duties. Washington dismissed them and sent them back to their home state.

In 1777 Congress organised four regiments of Continental Cavalry. These were based on the British Light Dragoon formations and a regiment consisted of six troops with sixty men in each. One dismounted troop was attached to each regiment to supply replacements and for other duties. There were three field officers to a regiment, a colonel, lieutenant-colonel and major, with each troop being commanded by a captain assisted by two lieutenants and a cornet. NCOs included one quartermaster sergeant, two sergeants and five corporals per troop with fifty privates, two trumpeters and a farrier. A private's pay was about 8·30 dollars per month.

The Cavalry were subjected to the same inadequacies of supply as the rest of the Army and as a result, rarely fulfilled a genuine cavalry function. Horses were always in short supply; at best each troop was usually able to put only 25 men in the saddle at any one time. There were even instances of whole troops being obliged to serve as foot soldiers for lack of mounts. Ironically, when horses were available the troopers were invariably wasted on courier and scouting duties rather than being engaged in harassing the enemy. Patriot Cavalry was at its most effective in the Southern campaigns under fine commanders like William Washington and Harry Lee.

5: Dress of the Cavalry

THE uniform coats of most of the larger bodies of Patriot Horse were much the same as those of the Infantry. Cavalry coats would often be shorter for ease in the saddle but this was by no means the rule. Facings varied throughout the War. In 1779 facings for American Cavalry were ordered to be white. In 1782 they were changed to red. Linings were either white or buff. Although boots were the accepted footwear for horse troops, many men, especially the Colonial Volunteer Cavalry, wore spatterdashes and shoes fitted with spurs. Breeches were buckskin and were often reinforced on the seat. The general pattern for headgear, apart from the inevitable cocked hats which many wore, was some form of leather helmet with either a feather or a fur roach for decoration. Often a turban was wound around the helmet which for the Provincial Cavalry was usually in the colour of their state. Later in the War some Cavalry changed to metal helmets but all retained the Light Dragoon look.

Horse equipment was of plain brown or black leather and saddle holsters had fur covered flaps. Very few troops had their distinctions marked on saddle cloths in the British manner, although the Philadelphia Light Horse were an exception to this. Capes or blankets were carried rolled behind the saddle. Scarcity of horses made uniformity of colour impossible and remounts would have been all shapes and sizes.

Rank distinctions for officers and NCOs were the same as in the Infantry. Trumpeters followed the practice of foot musicians in wearing coats of reversed colours with turnbacks of white or buff. Trumpets were brass, sometimes dressed in tassels and cords woven in the coat and facing colours, often with a metallic thread interwoven.

CAVALRY WEAPONS

Prominent Patriot horse officers, like Light Horse Harry Lee and William Washington regarded the sword as the classic cavalry weapon. They discouraged the use of firearms from the saddle, and seem to have found support among the Continental Cavalry as a whole. In a treatise on cavalry tactics a Captain Epaphras Hoyt of Massachusetts wrote, 'It is by the right use of the sword that they (the Americans) are to expect victory'. Weapons were always in short supply and the swords even in a single troop often varied considerably in appearance. The most common type of cavalry sword appears to have been metal hilted with a large pommel, single knuckle bow and quillon although some American Dragoons carried the double edged basket hilt sword with straight blade popular with horsemen of many armies at this period.

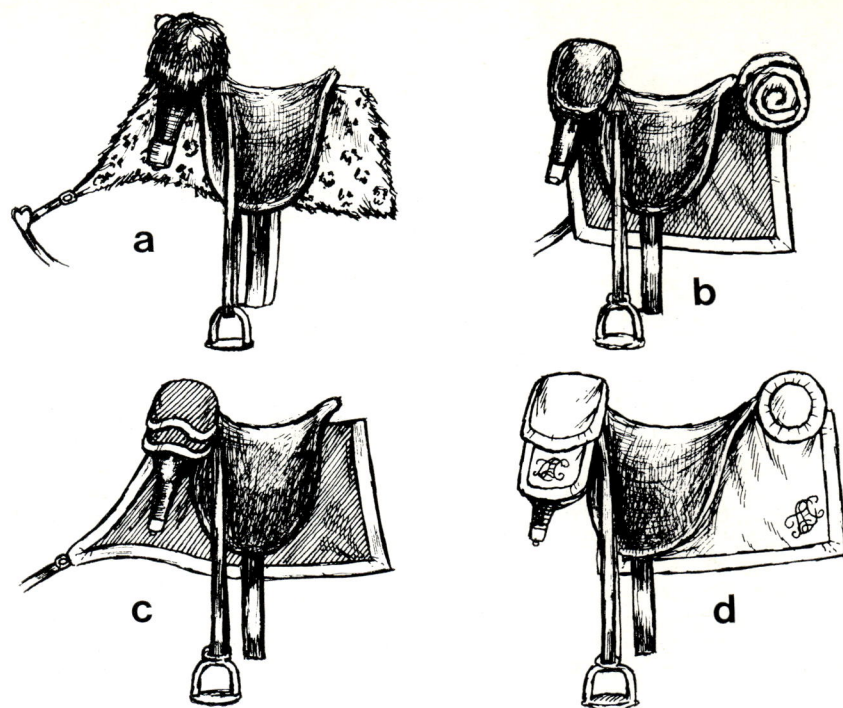

TYPES OF HORSE FURNITURE.
a. General Washington's Saddle. The holsters are sometimes
   shown without the fur covers.
b. Trooper's Saddle. 2nd Continental Dragoons.
   (Blue edged buff).
c. Senior Officer's Saddle. (Blue cloth edged with silver lace).
   Washington also used this type of saddle-cloth.
d. 1st City Troop of Philadelphia Light Horse. (Red brown with
   white edging and cypher for men, silver for officers).

When available carbines or muskets were carried on a shoulder
belt with a leather bucket on the right side of the saddle holding
the muzzle. Bayonets were also often worn by Cavalry. The saddle
holsters carried whatever pistols the horsemen could procure.

(OPPOSITE PAGE) CAVALRY SWORDS.
a. Officer's Sabre with pierced guard and wood grip.
b. Sabre with triple bar brass hilt, and wood grip.
c. Straight basket hilt sword popular with many American Dragoons.
   Iron hilt and bone grip. Double edge. Overall length 40 in.
d. Sabre 1750-80. Brass hilt. Single edge slightly curved blade.
   Approx 34 in. length.
e. Sabre 1775-85. Steel hilt curved single edged blade.
   Approx 33 in. length.
f. Dragoon of Virginia Sabre. 1778-90. Imported French blade on
   American hilt. Wood grip and pierced guard. Curved blade.
   Overall length 42 in.
g. Eagle head Horseman's sword 1780-1800. Brass hilt.

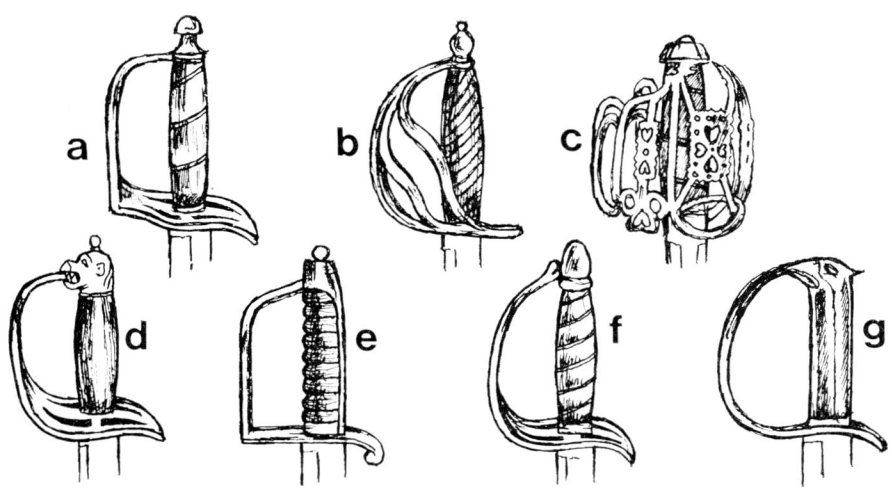

At Hobkirk's Hill on April 25, 1781, a miscalculation by the American commander Greene enabled the British force under Lord Rawdon to win the day. This print shows Patriot cavalry covering the American retreat. The troopers are wearing one of the many variations of the crested leather helmet.

a b c

d e f g

41

6: Cavalry Regiments

THE four Continental Cavalry Regiments organised in 1777 were clothed as follows:

1st CONTINENTAL DRAGOONS (BLAND'S)

Originally raised in Virginia as Provincial Light Dragoons in 1775 they joined Washington's army in December of that year. At that time there were six troops of The Virginia Horse under Major Bland. Some companies were dressed in blue coats faced red and with red waistcoats while others wore brown coats faced green. They had leather breeches and topboots and at this time wore leather helmets with black turbans and white horsehair crests. Later the helmets were altered to brass or steel with bearskin turbans and black or white horsehair crests. After 1777 when the Virginia Horse became the 1st Continental Dragoons carbines on shoulder belts were added to the armament of sabres and pistols. In 1780 Colonel Anthony White was the Commanding Officer but eventually the regiment was consolidated with the 3rd Cavalry under Lieutenant Colonel William Washington. Their full dress uniform now consisted of blue coats faced white, but in action white rifle shirts were worn over the regimentals.

2nd CONTINENTAL DRAGOONS (SHELDON'S)

This regiment wore a helmet similar to that worn by the 1st Dragoons but with a mid-blue turban in place of the bearskin. The helmet visors may have been leather and removable, although Trumbull's painting of the surrender at Saratoga shows a dragoon in the facing colour of this regiment wearing a helmet with a brass visor. Coats were blue with buff facings and white linings and buttons were of yellow metal as opposed to the white metal of the other dragoon regiments. Waistcoat and breeches were buff and equipment was as for other cavalry. The saddle cloth shown by Trumbull is dark blue with a buff border. In 1780 the shortage of mounts obliged some of this regiment to serve in an infantry capacity with overalls replacing breeches and boots.

3rd CONTINENTAL DRAGOONS (BAYLOR'S)

This regiment was also known as Lady Washington's Dragoons. Principally the men were recruited from the horse raising areas of Maryland and Virginia although one troop was formed in Pennsylvania. The famous cavalry leader, William Washington, took command of this regiment and led it in actions in the south coming up against his

42

British counterpart, Colonel Banastre Tarleton and his Loyalist Horse. The 3rd wore black leather peaked caps with red turbans (often with a white or yellow cord around) and either a bucktail or brown horsehair crest. Coats were white with medium blue facings and waistcoat, and white buttons. Breeches were white or buff as were the shoulder belts (although Peale in his portrait of William Washington shows a black shoulder belt). Swords were carried either on shoulder or waist belts and white sheepskins sometimes covered saddles.

4th CONTINENTAL DRAGOONS (MOYLAN'S)

The first uniforms of this regiment were red Infantry coats with blue facings captured from the British. It follows that if these coats were worn as they were taken, regimental lace would be in evidence on lapels and cuffs. The troopers covered these coats with hunting shirts in engagements where confusion with the British was likely. In 1779 the 4th Dragoons received their own distinctive uniform. The short coat was green faced red with red shoulder straps and turnbacks. Waistcoats were red and breeches buff. The head-dress consisted of a peaked leather helmet with a bearskin crest and sometimes a white turban. Later a brass helmet without peak with fur turban and white horsehair crest was substituted. A green cloak with a red cape was also issued to this regiment.

Apart from these four regiments, the Americans were served by numerous Provincial Troops of Horse raised by zealous patriots. The uniforms of these troops were so varied that it would be impossible to state categorically who wore what, where. The following list gives some of the facts that are known about a few of these Provincial Regiments and are typical of many others:

1st CITY TROOP OR PHILADELPHIA LIGHT HORSE

This troop acted as Washington's bodyguard from Philadelphia to New York in June, 1775, as he made his way to Cambridge. The uniform consisted of a reddish-brown coat faced and lined white with white buttons and waistcoat and white or buff breeches and belts. Black topboots were worn. The helmet of the troop was a leather jockey cap with a bucktail crest attached at the back of the helmet and fastened over the top to the centre point. A silver chain or braid surrounded the base of the cap. The troop had a saddle cloth, saddle roll and holsters of reddish-brown edged with white and with the letters 'L R' interwoven on the holsters and rear corner of the saddle cloth. The Philadelphia Light Horse were part of the Pennsylvania Militia who fought at Trenton and Princeton.

2nd REGIMENT OF CONNECTICUT LIGHT HORSE (CONNECTICUT MILITIA)

This was one of the many Light Horse Companies raised in Connecticut during the Revolution. The dress of Captain James Green's Troop consisted of a cocked hat fitted inside with a protective iron skull-cap. The coat was brown faced buff with white breeches and waistcoat. If boots were not available spatterdashes and shoes fitted with spurs were worn. An additional reason for the wearing of shoes could be that if the troop served in a true dragoon capacity (ie, fighting on foot after riding to the engagement) shoes would be more practical than boots. Equipment included a long carbine on buff shoulder belt with the muzzle resting in a leather bucket attached to the saddle, a sabre on a waistbelt and pistols in saddle holsters. Some of the companies of Connecticut Light Horse wore helmets of jacked leather.

THE SOUTH CAROLINA LIGHT HORSE

This unit wore a dress similar to The South Carolina Infantry which consisted of short blue coats with white facings and white metal buttons, a leather helmet with metal crescent on the front and either a bucktail or plume for decoration. The troopers were reputed to be well equipped in armament and horse furnishings.

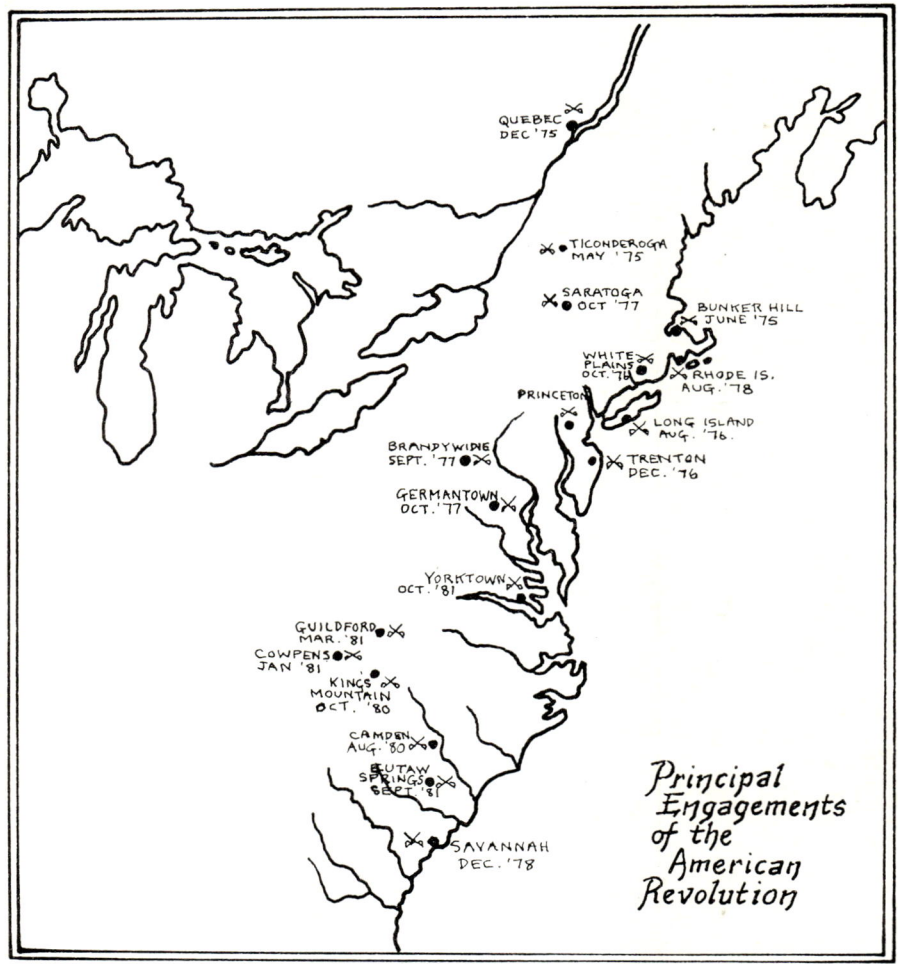

Principal Engagements of the American Revolution

7: Artillery

UNLIKE the Cavalry, Washington's Artillery was used to maximum effect for the greater part of the War. The Patriots were fortunate in having a fine Artillery commander in Henry Knox. Before the Revolution Knox had been an amateur gunnery enthusiast serving with a Massachusetts volunteer battery and now he brought all his expertise to work in organising the new American Artillery. Considering the deficiencies of supply the success achieved by Knox was considerable.

The American Artillery, at the outbreak of the War, was made up of corps of independent companies from all over the colonies. This persisted well into 1776 when four regiments of Continental Artillery were raised. By 1778 the first three of these regiments comprised twelve companies each and the fourth comprised eight companies. By 1780 re-organisation had established ten companies for each regiment. A company of Artillery was responsible for serving between eight and ten guns of assorted calibres. The men were assigned to the guns only for the duration of a particular operation. The only batteries organised on a permanent basis were light calibre Galloper guns usually pulled by one or two horses in single file. Light pieces were also often pulled by manpower. Guns of heavier calibres were towed by horses harnessed in pairs with anything up to four pairs per gun. The Artillery and its accompanying train were moved by civilian drivers, hired or pressed into service by the Army.

The guns Knox had to work with were of many types and calibres. They included twenty-four, eighteen, twelve, eight and four pounders and ranged from old British colonial pieces to naval guns taken from captured British vessels. Eventually, however, the Americans produced a considerable amount of their own artillery. Foundries were set up throughout the colonies, some of the more notable being the Durham Iron Works, which turned out small swivel cannon, barrels and cannon-balls, and the Warwick and Cornwall Furnaces of Pennsylvania. It was here during 1776 that sixty twelve and eighteen pounders were cast and soon afterwards America's first home-cast four pounders. Howitzers and mortars were also manufactured in quantity. The home of Continental cannon manufacture was chosen by Knox to be Springfield, Massachusetts. After the alliance with France in 1778, good French guns and powder were brought across for the Americans.

The most common calibres were four, eight and twelve pound solid shot cannon. These were used to batter down fortifications or break up massed Infantry. The effective range was up to about one mile. The guns also fired grape (large iron pellets) and cannister shot (small leaden balls). These were held in or around a metal body which broke up at the muzzle of the gun on discharge and scattered the contents. They were heavier than solid shot and effective only at close range.

Howitzers were lighter and shorter than cannon of corresponding calibre and were normally classed by diameter of bore rather than weight of shot.

In a pitched battle the guns were usually placed either between or in front of battalions of Infantry. The front position had the advantage of being able to protect the flanks of the foot soldiers. Elevation was measured by means of a quadrant placed in the muzzle and the procedure and drill orders for firing was as follows:

1. 'TEND VENT - SPONGE PIECE'. The touchhole was covered by a gunner's thumb while the piece was being loaded. The thumb was protected by a leather stool.

2. 'HANDLE CARTRIDGE'. A shot and powder bag was taken from the side box which was placed by the trails and carried to the muzzle. (The side boxes would normally be clamped to the axles of the gun carriage).

3. 'CHARGE PIECE - RAM DOWN CARTRIDGE'. The load was pushed down the barrel with a rammer.

4. 'PRIME'. The shot bag was pierced through the touchhole with a vent pick and a priming tube (usually a reed filled with powder) was pushed into the charge.

5. 'TAKE AIM'. The gun was re-sighted.

6. 'FIRE'. The slow match on the linstock was applied to the touchhole and the gun fired. Recoil was braked by ropes on the axle hooks and trails, and the gun rolled back into position. The barrel was cleared of burnt matter by means of a worm (a corkscrew-like implement) and the gun was sponged out for the next shot.

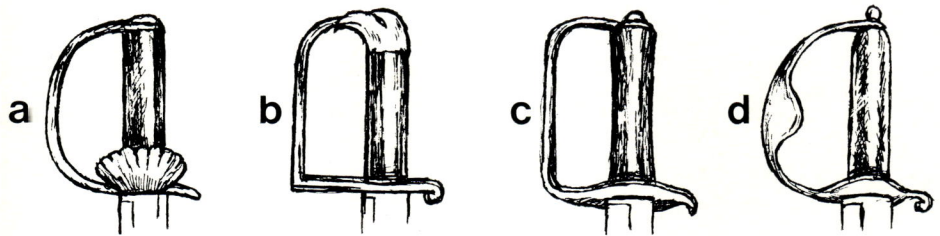

ARTILLERY SWORDS AND CUTLASSES.

a. Sabre with shell guard. (Approx. 32 in. overall length).

b. Hanger with eagle head pommel.

c. Cutlass with wooden grip. (Approx. 30 in. overall length).

d. Cutlass of British Naval Pattern. All iron hilt.
(Approx. 33 in. overall length).

8: Dress of the Artillery

BEFORE the establishment of four regiments of Continental Artillery in 1776, some of the independent companies were uniformed as follows:

LAMB'S NEW YORK ARTILLERY COMPANY: In 1775 this company wore a blue coat with buff facings and white linings. Waistcoats and breeches were white or buff and all buttons were pewter. The cocked hat had no edging lace. Black spatterdashes were worn over the white stockings. A second company was similarly clothed and known as

THE COLONY ARTILLERY COMPANY: These New York units provided the nucleus of the 2nd Continental Artillery Regiment in 1776.

THE MASSACHUSETTS ARTILLERY REGIMENT: This unit was established in 1775. At first the gunners were not uniformed although the officers were well dressed at their own expense in blue coats faced red and lined white with the lapel buttons set in pairs and trimmed with gold lace around the buttonholes. The hats also had gold lace trim and the smallclothes were white with black boots. Crimson waist sashes and gilt epaulettes were worn and spontoons were carried on parade. By 1778 all ranks were well uniformed and the regiment had become part of the 3rd Continental Artillery. Attached to them was Major Ebenezer Stevens' Independent Battery of Artillery similarly clothed.

The four Continental Artillery regiments of 1777 were dressed in the following uniform:

'A blue or black coat reaching to the knee and full trimmed, lappels fastened back, with ten open worked buttonholes in yellow silk on the breast of each lappel and ten large regimental yellow buttons at equal distances on each side. Three large yellow regimental buttons on each cuff and a like number on each pocket flap. The skirts to hook back showing the red lining. Bottom of coat cut square, red lappels, cuff linings and standing capes (collar), single-breasted white waistcoat with twelve small yellow regimental buttons, white breeches, black half-gaiters, white stock ruffled shirt and at the wrists and black cocked hat bound with yellow, red plume and black cockade. Gilt handled small sword and gilt epaulettes'. (Officers only.)

The General Order of October, 1779 confirmed these details but added mention of coats 'edged with narrow lace or tape', presumably lapels and cuffs. No change in dress was made in the Order of December 6, 1782, or after the reductions at the end of the War when only two companies of Artillery were retained.

THE RHODE ISLAND TRAIN OF ARTILLERY: This was part of Rhode

Island's contribution to the Army of New England before Boston in 1775. Its Captain, John Crane, was promoted Major and during the first year of the War the regiment was a separate command from the Boston Artillery Regiment. On re-organisation in 1776 Crane became Colonel of the 3rd Continental Artillery and the coats of brown faced red worn by the Rhode Islanders were changed to the regulation blue faced red. The cap of the Train in 1775 was a distinctive one made up from six pieces of jacked leather sewn together to form a cone and with a curious hooked leather front bearing a gold anchor shaded dark red and with a red scroll above bearing the motto in gold, 'FOR OUR COUNTRY'. Below the anchor was a second red scroll with the words, 'IN TE DOMINE SPERAMUS' in gold. A small brass button at each side of the cap bore the anchor of Rhode Island as did the coat buttons. This uniform was worn by all ranks, the privates wearing spatterdashes in place of the officers' boots. Muskets were carried when the Artillerymen were not serving the guns. Officers wore a gilt epaulette, crimson sash, sabre and carried a spontoon on parade.

REPRESENTATION OF AN AMERICAN FLOATING BATTERY (from a contemporary English Manuscript). In September 1775 two floating batteries were launched in the Charles River, Massachusetts. Shortly afterwards they were in action firing on the British in Boston. A heavy gun was positioned at each end and smaller guns at the after quarters. The plank sides were pierced for musket fire and oars, and four swivel guns were mounted on top. For flag details see Section 10, page 67.

Left to right: PRIVATE: LAFAYETTE LIGHT INFANTRY 1781.
LIEUTENANT: 2nd CANADIAN REGT (CONGRESS'S OWN). 1778
CAPTAIN: SHERBURNE'S CONTINENTAL REGT 1779.
DRUMMER 1st NEW YORK REGT 1780

9: Engineers and other Services

LITTLE thought was given to specialised engineering in the early years of the Revolution. Infantry or Artillery officers in command of an operation either handled the field works themselves or appointed the most competent man under them. It was the influence of the French that established the basis for the American Engineer Corps. Men like Duportail and Koscuiszko brought to the Patriots their experience in the theory and practice of military engineering. The establishment of 1778 made provision for three companies in the Engineer Corps, each containing sixty men. It said that they were 'to be instructed in the fabrication of field works, as far as relates to the manual or mechanical part. Their business shall be to instruct the fatigue parties to do their duties with celerity and exactness, to repair injuries done to the works by the enemies' fire and to prosecute works in the face of it'. The headquarters of the Engineers were at West Point.

DRESS OF THE ENGINEERS

The Corps of Engineers, Sappers and Miners were ordered to wear 'blue coats with buff facings and red linings, buff underclothes (waistcoat and breeches) and epaulettes of their respective ranks. (Headquarters, Short Hills, June 18, 1780.) A further order of December, 1782 reaffirmed these uniform colours. As so many foreign advisers served among the American Engineers one would expect a number of European uniforms to be evident amongst the blue and buff coats.

MEDICAL SERVICES

In May 1775 the Massachusetts Provincial Congress appointed the first Patriot Army medical board. Dr Benjamin Church was made the first Director General Chief Physician of the first Army hospital but disgraced himself by dealing with the enemy and was consequently removed from office being replaced by a Dr John Morgan. Morgan held the position until 1777 when Dr William Shippen took his place. Shippen served until 1781, his duties then being taken over by Dr John Cochran who filled the post until the end of the War.

All the army physicians were handicapped by lack of money and medical supplies and the inexperience of their subordinates. They did however manage to give a reasonable hospital service to the Patriots notwithstanding. Wards built in Indian style huts were organised and appear to have been heated and ventilated in a style far in advance of contemporary medical thinking.

NAVY AND MARINES

The history of the American Navy dates from December, 1775. In September of that year the Marine Committee of the Continental Congress uniformed the men following these regulations:

Captains	-	Blue coat with red lapels, slashed cuffs, a stand up collar, flat yellow buttons, blue breeches, red waistcoat with yellow lace.
Lieutenants	-	Blue coat, red lapels, round cuffs faced, a stand up collar, yellow buttons, blue breeches and plain red waistcoat.
Masters	-	Blue coat with lapels, round cuffs, blue breeches and red waistcoat.
Midshipmen	-	Blue coat with lapels, round cuffs faced red, stand up collar, red at the buttons and buttonholes, blue breeches red waistcoat.
Marines	-	Green coat faced white, round cuffs slashed sleeves and pockets with buttons round the cuffs, silver epaulette on the right shoulder, skirts turned back, buttons to suit the facings, white waistcoat, breeches edged with green, black gaiters and garters. (The men had green shirts if these could be procured.)
Common sailors and seamen	-	Loose breeches and short square cut jackets.

The rattlesnake emblem was frequently associated with the Navy and often worn as a badge on epaulettes. The head-dress of the Navy was a cocked hat for officers and a tarred leather or stocking cap for seamen. Marines wore a small round hat braided white and turned up at the left side with a cockade. After 1779 the facings and linings of Marine uniforms were altered from white to red. Marines wore white waistcoats, breeches and stockings with buckled shoes. Rank markings were as for the Infantry. Some Infantry soldiers were detached from land duty to serve as marines by a General Order of July, 1776, when the fleet was forming on Lake Champlain.

The Continental Navy had only about 73 vessels and 260 officers throughout the War. Although greatly outnumbered by both men and ships of the British Navy they managed to fight some very successful actions under men such as John Paul Jones. Much of Knox's artillery was made up of guns captured by the Patriot Navy at sea and adapted for use in land engagements.

Left to right: PRIVATE: GOVERNOR'S FOOTGUARDS OF CONNECTICUT. 1775.
RIFLEMAN: MORGAN'S RIFLES. 1776.
MARINE: CONTINENTAL MARINES. 1780.
CAPTAIN: CONTINENTAL NAVY. 1776.

Left to right: CAPTAIN: 1st CONTINENTAL DRAGOONS. 1777.
TROMPETER: 3rd CONTINENTAL DRAGOONS. 1777
TROOPER: 4th CONTINENTAL DRAGOONS. 1779.
TROOPER: 2nd CONTINENTAL DRAGOONS. 1777

10: American Colours

AT the outbreak of the Revolution the patriotic fervour prompted the populace to bring out all types of flags. The new soldiers were following banners of towns, counties, militia units and not a few individual slogans of defiance and liberty were in evidence. Even when the initial enthusiasm settled down to something more rational each colony, regiment and even company was marching behind some Colour or other.

On January 1, 1776, the Great or Grand Union Flag was raised near Washington's headquarters at Cambridge. It was also known as the Cambridge Flag and consisted of seven red and six white horizontal stripes with the British Union Flag in the first canton. It is not known whether this flag was officially adopted by Congress but it was soon being called the Congress or Continental Flag. It was intended more as a flag for use on forts or ships than one to be carried in action.

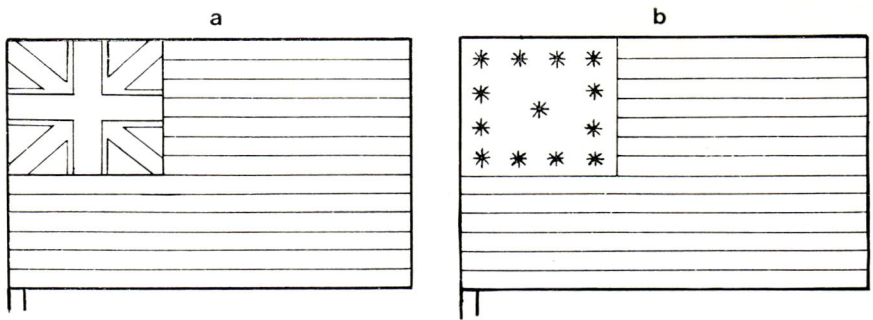

a. *The Grand Union Flag. (Cambridge Flag).*
b. *The first Stars and Stripes (after Trumbull).*

This flag was replaced in June, 1777, by one of the same number of stripes but with the first canton occupied by a blue field bearing a constellation of thirteen white stars. This flag was officially adopted by a resolution of the Continental Congress and was reputedly carried for the first time in action at an engagement fought in Delaware on September 3 of that year. It was definitely on the field at Brandywine in Chester County, Pennsylvania, eight days later. If the evidence of contemporary artists is to be believed then this flag had quite a number of variations of design. Trumbull's two paintings, one of the battle of Princeton and the other of Burgoyne's surrender at Saratoga show twelve stars around the edge of the blue canton with one in the centre. The same flag in a portrait of Washington by Peale however shows the thirteen stars in the more familiar circle arrangement. Correspondence dated as late as May, 1779 indicates that even at that time the final pattern for a national flag had not been settled.

'The Board have been frequently applied to on the Subject of Drums and Colours for the several Regiments. It is impossible to comply with all the Requisitions for these Articles, as we have not materials to make either in sufficient Numbers. We hope however to have in a short Time a competent Number of Drums. So soon as they are made we send them to Camp as we find many Irregularities and Inconveniences arise from delivering them or any other Articles here.

As to Colours we have refused them for another Reason. The Baron Steuben mentioned when he was here that he would settle with your Excellency some Plan as to the Colours. It was intended that every Regiment should have two Colours one the Standard of the United States which should be the same throughout the Army and the other a Regimental Colour which should vary according to the facings of the Regiments. But it is not yet settled what is the Standard of the U. States. If your Excellency will therefore favor us with your opinion on the Subject we will report to Congress and request them to establish a Standard and so soon as this is done we will endeavour to get Materials and order a Number made sufficient for the Army. Neither can we tell what should be the Regimental Colours as the Uniforms were by a late Resolution of Congress to be settled by your Excellency'. (War Board letter.)

Many of the colonies had their own symbols which were used in one form or another throughout the War as a decoration for Colours. Massachusetts had the pine tree, New York a beaver, Rhode Island an anchor, etc.

The following section gives descriptions of the few American Colours which have survived or details of which have been handed down.

NEW HAMPSHIRE

The 2nd New Hampshire Regiment had two flags. The first called the blue flag measured five feet along the staff and five feet six inches on the fly. The red shield in the centre of the flag was beneath three golden scrolls bearing the words, 'THE GLORY NOT THE PREY'. The shield bore the interwoven initials 'NH' with '2nd' below this and 'REGT' below this again. The first canton bore two superimposed crosses, the vertical red edged gold and the diagonal gold edged red. The flag had a fine gold fringe.

The second of the flags, called the buff flag, had a golden sun in the centre emitting thirteen rays and thirteen lines from it. The sun bore the motto 'WE ARE ONE'. Surrounding this sun were thirteen linked golden rings each bearing the name of a colony. In the first canton the white crosses were on a ground of eight triangles alternately

[continued on page 58]

Left to right: TROOPER: THE VIRGINIA HORSE. 1775.
TROOPER: SOUTH CAROLINA LIGHT HORSE. 1777
TROOPER: 2nd CONNECTICUT LIGHT HORSE. 1776.
TROOPER: 1st CITY TROOP. PHILADELPHIA LIGHT HORSE. 1775

Left to right: MATROSS: CONTINENTAL ARTILLERY 1779
LIEUTENANT: RHODE ISLAND TRAIN OF ARTILLERY 1775
PRIVATE: CONTINENTAL LIGHT INFANTRY. 1783
PRIVATE: HASLETT'S DELAWARE REGT 1777

[continued from page 55]
red and pale blue. This flag was the same size as the previous one.

Both of these flags were captured by the 9th Foot at Fort Anne two months before Saratoga.

MASSACHUSETTS

Many Massachusett's Colours carried variations of the colony's pine tree symbol, sometimes with the motto 'AN APPEAL TO HEAVEN' or 'AN APPEAL TO GOD'. The Bunker Hill flag had a red ground (some authorities say blue) with a white first canton bearing a red plus cross and with a small green pine tree in the corner. Another type of pine tree flag shown in Trumbull's painting of Bunker Hill has a red field with a white first canton bearing a large green pine tree.

The flag of the Bedford Minute Men measured approximately two feet square and had a dark red ground bearing a silver arm holding a sword and coming out of a series of silver discs. To the right of

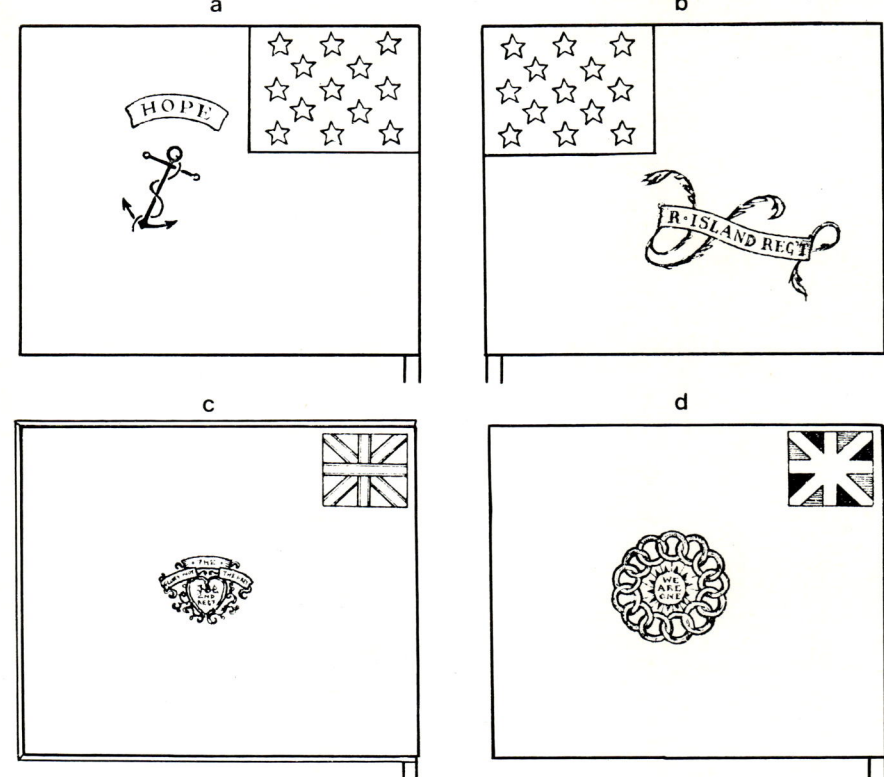

PATRIOT INFANTRY COLOURS.
a. Flag of the 1st. Rhode Island Regt.
b. Flag of the 2nd. Rhode Island Regt.
c. Blue flag of the 2nd New Hampshire Regt.
d. Buff flag of the 2nd New Hampshire Regt.

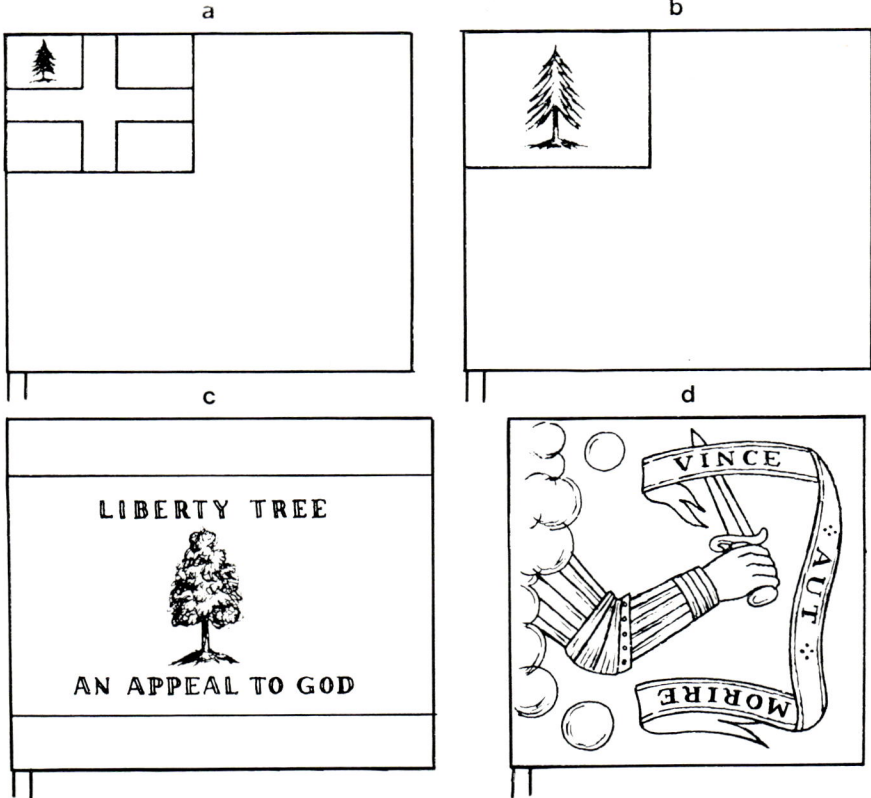

PATRIOT FLAGS OF MASSACHUSETTS.
a. The Bunker Hill Flag.
b. The Bunker Hill flag (after Trumbull).
c. The Liberty Tree flag.
d. Flag of the Bedford Minute Men.

the arm was a scroll in gold bearing the motto, 'VINCE AUT MORIRE'. This flag was originally designed in England in the 1660s as a standard for the County Troop of Middlesex, Suffolk and Essex. It was originally fringed silver around the edge. The flag was carried by the Bedford Men in the action at Concord Bridge.

The flag of the 13th Massachusett's Infantry Regiment appears to have been a rather ornate affair. Unfortunately only a sketchy description of it is available. The flag is given as a light buff ground with a pine tree and a field of Indian corn. Two officers in the uniform of the regiment appear on the flag, one wounded in the breast with blood streaming from the wound. Under the pine tree are several children. One of the officers is pointing to them. The flag also bears the motto, 'FOR POSTERITY I BLEED'.

[continued on page 62]

Left to right: PRIVATE: DE LANCEY'S BRIGADE. 1776.
PRIVATE: THE KING'S ORANGE RANGERS. 1781.
PRIVATE: BUTLER'S RANGERS. 1778.
PRIVATE: JOHNSON'S ROYAL GREENS. 1776.

Left to right: HUSSAR: THE QUEEN'S RANGERS. 1780.
TROOPER: THE KING'S AMERICAN DRAGOONS. 1782.
TROOPER: EMMERICH'S MOUNTED CHASSEURS. 1776.
OFFICER: TARLETON'S BRITISH LEGION. 1780.

RHODE ISLAND

The flag of the 1st Rhode Island Regiment measured six and a half feet on the fly and five feet on the staff. It was a white flag with thirteen gold stars on the mid blue canton. In the centre of the flag was a blue anchor and above this a blue scroll with the word, 'HOPE' in white. The regiment served at Trenton, Brandywine and Yorktown.

The flag of the 2nd Rhode Island Regiment was also white silk with thirteen white stars on the blue canton. The centre of the flag bore a blue scroll with white lettering reading, 'R. ISLAND REG'T'. The two regiments were consolidated in 1780 and fought in many engagements. In 1784 the two flags were presented to the state of Rhode Island.

CONNECTICUT

In April of 1775 troops from Connecticut adopted the motto, 'QUI TRANSTULIT SUSTINET' to affix to their standards and drums. In the same month the Provincial Congress of the colony ordered the raising of six regiments with a distinguishing standard of a different colour for each of the six. The colours were as follows:

1st Regiment	-	Yellow
2nd Regiment	-	Blue
3rd Regiment	-	Scarlet (with the 'APPEAL TO HEAVEN' motto on one side and 'QUI TRANSTULIT SUSTINET' on the other)
4th Regiment	-	Crimson
5th Regiment	-	White
6th Regiment	-	Azure

On July 1, 1775, two other regiments were ordered to be raised their colours being blue for the 7th and orange for the 8th.

A regulation for regimental colours in the Connecticut line dated September, 1780 is as follows:

'The ground of each to be different—each to bear the number of the Regt. in large characters:—the devise on one side, the Connt. Arms —on the other, the devise and motto of the 30 Dollar Bills. If the ground of two colours should be so alike as not to be distinguishable 3 or 400 yards, a small field of 13 stripes in the Lower Quarter of one of them may serve as a distinction'.

The flag of Webb's Regiment (3rd Connecticut) was approximately three feet six inches on the fly by three feet on the staff. Its colouring was a yellow ground bearing a white sword and green branches tied with a red ribbon. The numeral '1' in black perhaps indicated the first company.

Some details of the Regimental Colour of this same regiment exist. They are of a flag made of yellow silk and bearing across the top a blue scroll with the inscription, 'IN MERIDIEM PROGRED ET . . .' (here the flag was damaged and the rest of the inscription was obliterated). Below this scroll was a rather complex design consisting of an Indian carrying a shield and sword and wearing a feather bonnet. He is also holding a staff (topped by a Quaker hat) which flies a red and white striped forktail banner. To the right of the Indian stands a dog-like animal. At its feet lie a crown and a head, presumably the King's, pierced by an arrow.

Webb's Regiment was raised in 1780 from the 2nd and 9th Regiments.

Although in the Orders of the Connecticut Congress the colour of the flag for the 2nd Regiment is designated as blue, the actual flag for the 2nd battalion of this regiment was in fact dark red. It could be that the discrepancy arose from some Connecticut Militia unit bringing its Colours into the Continental Army during one of the many amalgamations which took place throughout the War.

The red silk flag which measured approximately four feet on the fly by three on the staff bore large letters in gold indicating the battalion, regiment and colony. The other side was decorated with a red shield surrounded by a scroll bearing a gold motto. The shield was surmounted by a bright blue ribbon and had round its edge a bright blue border. On the shield were three golden vines. The motto was an abbreviation of the usual Connecticut 'QUI TRAN . . etc. .'.

The flag was in the possession of a Colonel John Mix who at one time had been Adjutant of the 2nd Regiment of Connecticut Line. He deposited the flag in the state arsenal before his death in 1834.

*Obverse and reverse of the flag of the
2nd Battalion, 2nd Regiment of Connecticut Infantry
(the 1640 probably refers to an earlier parent unit).*

NEW YORK

In the early days of the War a common flag carried by many New York companies was the State's black beaver on a white field.

The flag of the 3rd New York Regiment measured approximately six feet on the fly by about five feet on the staff. It consisted of an adaptation of the State Arms (see colour plate for details). The flag was made in either 1778 or 1779 and is known to have been at Yorktown. The 3rd New York Regiment was commanded by Colonel Peter Gansevoort and was eventually consolidated with the 2nd New York Regiment.

PENNSYLVANIA

The flag of the 1st Pennsylvania (Continental) Line Regiment was carried by the regiment throughout the Revolution from Boston in 1775 to Yorktown in 1781. It consisted of a green field with a centre

A

B

C

D

E

F

PATRIOT FLAGS

A. INDEPENDENT BATT. WESTMORELAND COUNTY, PENN.
C. 3rd NEW YORK REGIMENT.
E. COMMANDER-IN-CHIEF'S GUARD.

B. 1st CITY TROOP, PHILADELPHIA LIGHT HORSE.
D. 1st PENNSLYLVANIA (CONTINENTAL) LINE REGIMENT.
F. HANOVER ASSOCIATION OF LANCASTER COUNTY, PE

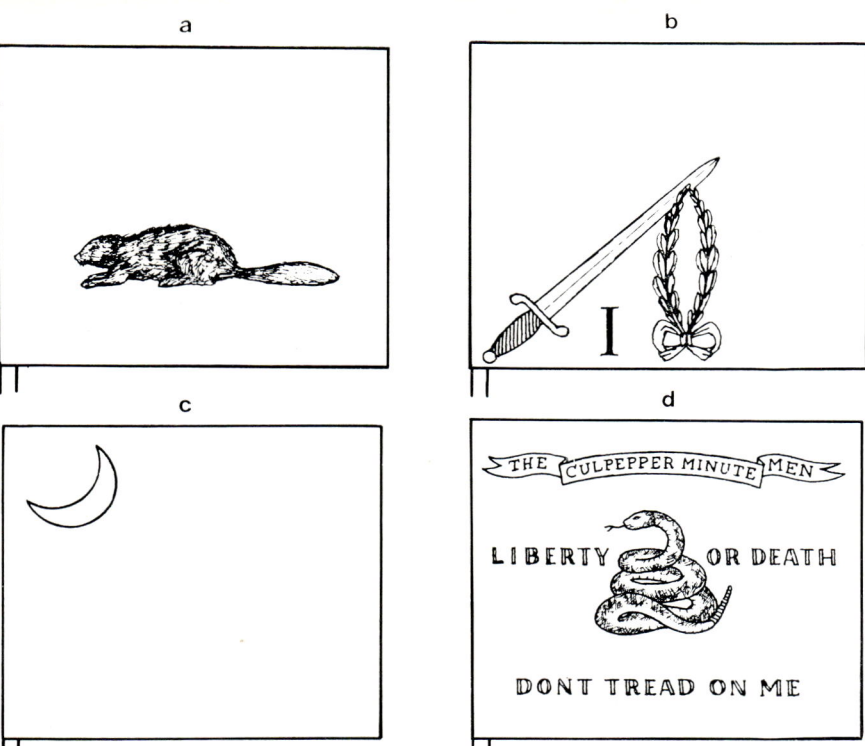

PATRIOT COLOURS.
a. Beaver flag of New York State.
b. 3rd. Connecticut Regt. (Webb's) 1780.
c. Crescent flag of South Carolina.
d. Flag of the Culpepper Minute Men of Virginia.

patch of red bearing figures of a hunter and lion. (See colour plate for details). The Motto, 'DOMARI NOLO' is translated as 'I refuse to be subjugated'.

The flag of the Hanover Association of Lancaster County, Pennsylvania consisted of a crimson field bearing a rifleman and scroll with motto (see colour plate for details).

The flag of the Independent Battalion, Westmoreland County, Pennsylvania was an old English ensign altered for use by the Patriots. It consisted of a Union flag in the first canton whilst the red field carried a variation of the popular rattlesnake motif (see colour plate for details). The flag was carried in many engagements including Trenton and Princeton.

VIRGINIA

The flag of the Culpepper Minute Men of Virginia was yet another rattlesnake design. It was a white flag with the snake and lettering in black. This company was part of a regiment commanded by Patrick Henry in 1775.

65

SOUTH CAROLINA

The crescent flag of South Carolina was the first American flag to be used in the south during the Revolution. The ground colour of blue was after the blue of the colony's uniforms and the silver crescent reflected the device on the soldiers' helmets. It was known as 'Moultrie's Blue Flag'.

South Carolina was the state in which the rattlesnake flag originated. It was designed and presented to Congress in February, 1776, by Colonel Gadsden and was intended as a flag for the Commander-in-Chief of the Navy. Among the many variations of the flag were those including the rattlesnake moving across a ground of thirteen horizontal red and blue or red and white stripes, often with the motto, 'DON'T TREAD ON ME' across the top or the bottom. Sometimes the snake was wrapped around a pine tree. The rattle often had thirteen rings symbolising the number of colonies.

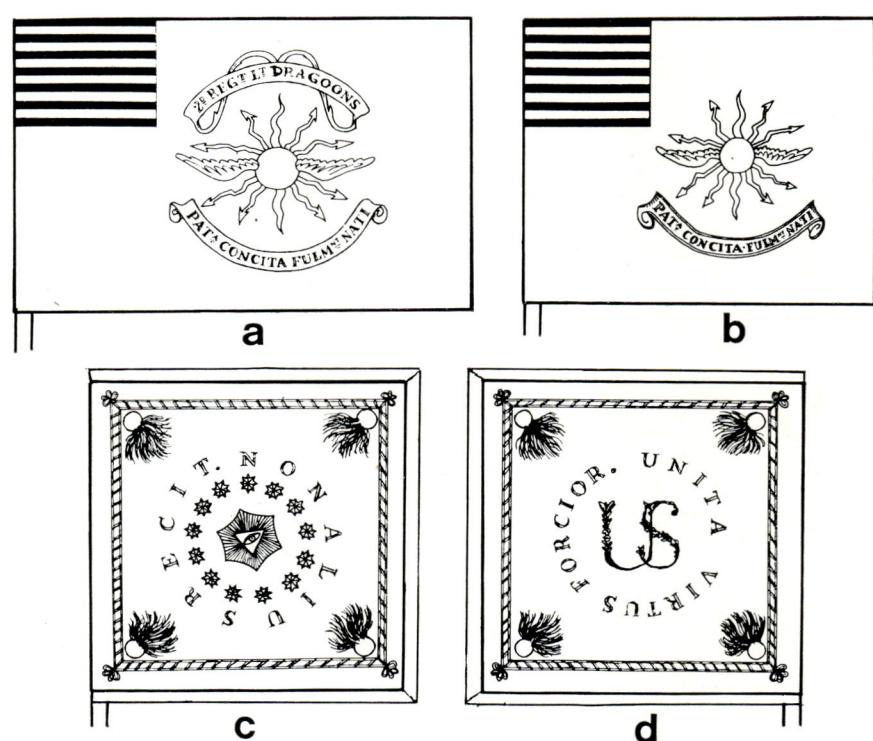

PATRIOT CAVALRY FLAGS.

a. Blue Standard of Talmadge's Troop of the
   2nd Continental Dragoons.
b. Pink Standard of the same Troop.
c. Banner of Pulaski's Legion.
d. Reverse of the same banner.

CAVALRY FLAGS

Details are known of two standards of Captain Talmadge's Troop of the 2nd Continental Dragoons. The first is a blue flag measuring approximately three and a half feet on the fly by two and a half feet on the staff. In the first canton is a blue silk patch with seven horizontal gold stripes sewn to it. In the centre of the flag is a blue disc with wings and thunderbolts in gold. The two scrolls on the flag are gold with black lettering.

The other flag is similar although pink in colour and measuring approximately two and a half feet square. The canton in this flag has six horizontal white stripes sewn on a pink patch and the centre design differs only from that of the blue flag in having silver wings and only one scroll, silver with black lettering.

The flag of Pulaski's Legion was an eighteen inch square, red banner with the design embroidered upon it in gold silk. This standard was carried by Pulaski's Troop until his death at Savannah, Georgia, in 1779. It was originally presented by a group of Patriot women known as the Moravian Sisters.

The flag of the 1st City Troop of Philadelphia Light Horse bore a horizontal striped canton with a coat of arms in the centre (see colour plate for details).

Exact details of the Eutaw flag carried by William Washington's Cavalry at Cowpens in 1781 are not known. It appears to have been a small, red, damask square ornamented with fringe and carried on a hickory pole. It was reputedly made for the troop by a lady friend of William Washington.

OTHER FLAGS

The flag of the Commander-in-Chief's Guard consisted of a white ground bearing a coloured pictorial motif and scroll in the centre. The scroll was green with the motto 'CONQUER OR DIE' in gold (see colour plate for details).

Washington's Command flag at Valley Forge was a mid blue ground bearing thirteen six-pointed stars.

In September 1775 two floating batteries were launched in the Charles river, Massachusetts. They were in action the following month firing on the enemy in Boston. They reputedly flew an ensign consisting of a white ground with a centre design of a green pine tree surmounted by the red motto, 'AN APPEAL TO HEAVEN'. The flag was edged with a gold fringe. Floating batteries of Pennsylvania on the Delaware river also carried this flag in the autumn of 1775 and again in the defence of Philadelphia in 1777 and 1778.

A flag carried at the Battle of White Plains on October 28, 1776 consisted of a white field bearing the motto, 'LIBERTY OR DEATH' and a pole topped with a liberty cap and crossing a sword. All markings were black. Another liberty flag was carried by the Patriots at the Battle of Long Island on August 26, 1776. This consisted of a dark red field with the word, 'LIBERTY' painted across it in white.

As well as the Continental Navy using many variations of the rattle-a

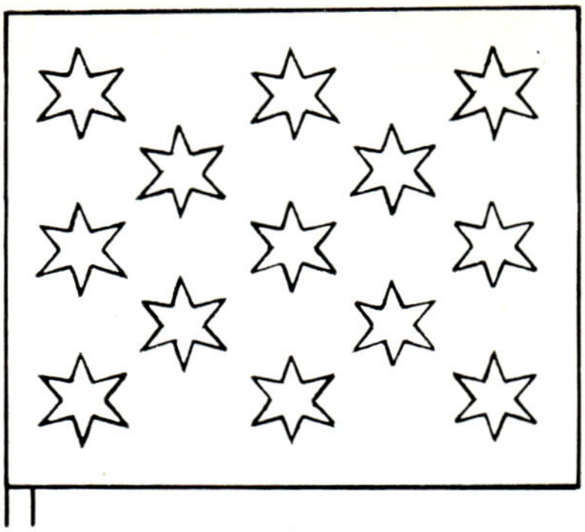

b

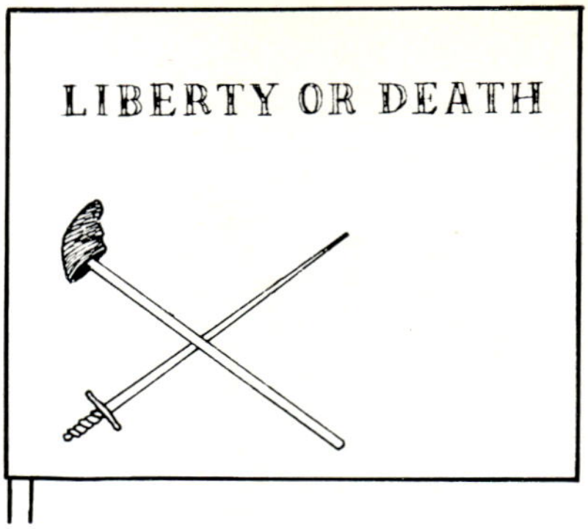
LIBERTY OR DEATH

c

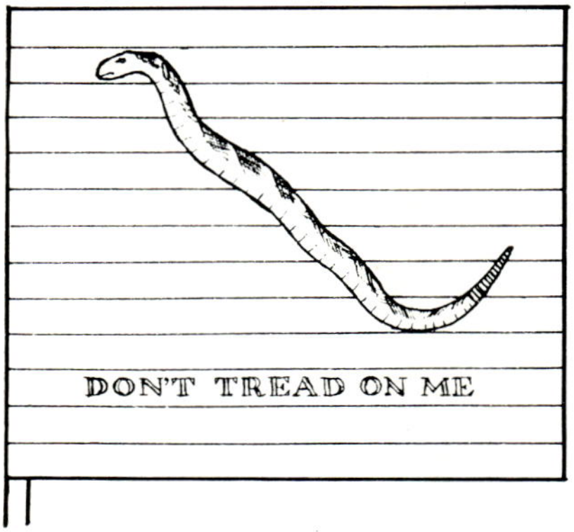
DON'T TREAD ON ME

d

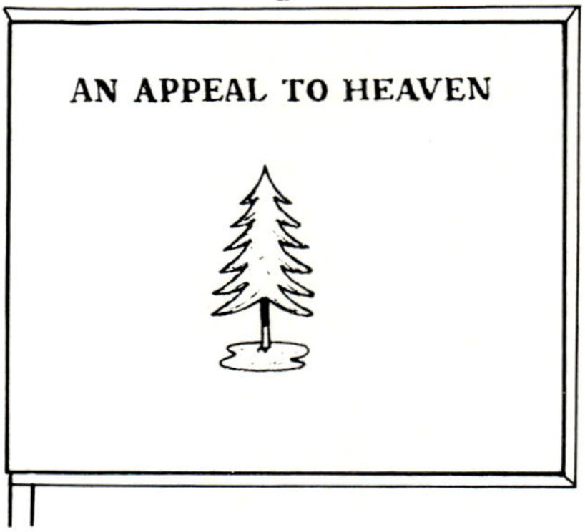
AN APPEAL TO HEAVEN

a. Washington's Command Flag at Valley Forge.

b. Liberty Flag carried at the Battle of White Plains, Oct. 28 1776.

c. One type of rattlesnake flag, used extensively by the Navy and many Militia units.

d. Flag of the Floating Batteries.

snake flag its privateers of the Revolution flew an ensign of thirteen horizontal yellow and black, or yellow and white stripes.

THE BUCKS OF AMERICA

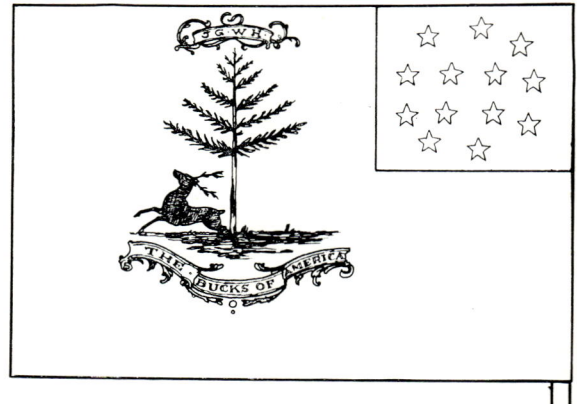

Flag of the Bucks of America, an organisation of Patriot Negroes.

Details are known of a flag which belonged to an organisation of Patriot Negroes called the Bucks of America. The flag measured approximately five feet on the fly by three and a half feet on the staff. The canton was blue with thirteen gilt stars and the buff flag bore in the centre a brown buck running under a tree of blue-green which grew from a blue-green plot. The scrolls above and below the motif were dark 'robin's egg blue' shaded with dark green and carried gilt letters.

Sergeant
Light Dragoons
of the
Queen's Rangers

Part Two
THE LOYALISTS

1: The Loyalist Cause

THE call for Independence after Lexington was by no means unanimous throughout the colonies. The American Revolution was as much a civil war as a struggle for liberty, with something like 60,000 American colonists remaining faithful to Great Britain. These colonists were known disdainfully by the Patriots as 'Tories', after Lord North and his colleagues in London, but they called themselves 'Loyalists', an open indication that they had no wish to be separated from the Crown.

Loyalists made up approximately one third of the population of the Thirteen Colonies and came from all walks of life. Most of the immigrant settlers from Britain had Loyalist sympathies and a great many more came from the more prosperous classes, such as merchants, lawyers, physicians, etc. Before the conflict many of these British sympathisers had held commissions in the Militia of the various states and they now found that the soldiers they had previously commanded openly disobeyed them. As a result the Officer Corps of the Militia was disbanded and elections held to allow the rank and file to choose their new leaders. This served to expel all anti-Whig factions and the new Militia, in general, was established on the side of the Patriots. The disbanded Loyalists either joined the British forces or raised their own Corps to fight alongside the British. Many wealthy and influential men donated large sums of money to furnishing the Loyalist cause. The De Lancey's of West Chester County, New York were one of many famous families involved in the Loyalist cause in this way. Another influential Loyalist, John Murray, Earl of Dunmore and Royal Governor of Virginia, raised two regiments in support of the British, The Queen's Own Loyal Virginians and a Negro corps, Lord Dunmore's Ethiopians. Both of these regiments saw active service.

The Loyalist faction was well distributed throughout the colonies. New York had a great number, as did New Jersey, Delaware and Maryland. Pennsylvania was extremely strong in Tory sympathies as were Connecticut and Vermont and in South Carolina the Loyalists outnumbered the Whigs. Even as late as 1781 Georgia was contemplating abandoning the struggle for independence because of the tremendous number of Tories in that state.

As with the Patriot Army the Loyalist troops were often unable to secure sufficient supplies. Typical was the case of Colonel David Fanning of South Carolina who, after raising a regiment of about 500 Loyalist volunteers was obliged to dismiss all but fifty of them because they could not be suitably equipped.

The struggle between the Loyalist and the Patriot was much more bloody than that between the latter and the British. The Patriots regarded all Loyalists as traitors and frequently gave no quarter or punished them severely, destroying Tory property. The least a captured Loyalist could expect to escape with was a tarring and feathering. British captives frequently enjoyed the basic privileges of prisoners of war while their Loyalist comrades were denied these benefits. Naturally, this prejudiced attitude of the Patriots only served to make the Loyalists more determined in their fight and caused them to punish their own prisoners with the same severity. A number of Loyalist corps, such as Butler's Rangers, are recorded as having waged war in a particularly barbarous manner. Atrocities, however, were not one-sided and can be brought into perspective to some extent remembering that both factions employed savage Indians in their campaigns.

Paradoxically, when the War ended, the defeated Tories were in the main treated quite fairly. Property and land were generally confiscated but there was very little of the bloodshed that was seen later in the century during the French Revolution. Many Loyalists, of course, left the colonies forever, either returning to Britain or establishing settlements in Canada.

A great number of the Loyalists corps were excellent soldiers but their forces lacked unity and in most cases were poorly led. If the British had drilled and instructed these willing volunteers in the use of arms then a powerful army could have been established and the Tory force would have been put to much better use.

Some of the Loyalists most usefully employed were those on naval duty. Rhode Island was foremost in furnishing many experienced seamen to operate convoys of transport ships. The Tory Navy was instrumental in supplying the British forces on numerous occasions and in capturing a number of guns from Patriot vessels. It was also involved in the transportation of landing parties.

2: Dress of the Loyalists

LIKE their Patriot opponents, the Loyalists who took up arms at the outbreak of the Revolution were inadequately uniformed and equipped. As yet no official uniforms were in use and often a company was identified solely by a device in the cap or a badge on the clothing. The Royal North British Volunteers raised in Boston in October, 1775, wore a blue bonnet with the cross of St Andrew upon it; a reminder of their Scottish origins. In the same city, one month later, more Loyalists were formed into three companies with a distinguishing badge of a sash tied around the left arm. These were called the Loyal American Association. The Tory Irish of Boston banded together as the Loyal Irish Volunteers, wearing a white cockade in their hats as a distinction.

Many of the immigrants from Scotland retained a major portion of their national dress. At the engagement at Moore's Creek Bridge in February 1776, the North Carolina Militia, mainly Scots who had come to America after the Jacobite rebellion, wore Highland dress and carried Scottish broadswords.

By 1776 the British Government was supplying the American Tories with uniforms and equipment. It was decided to clothe all Loyalist troops in green coats faced white, green or blue. Later, orange, red or black were added to the list of facing colours, the Colonel of a regiment to select the colour of his choice. Linings were usually white.

In 1778, with a few exceptions, the colour of regimental coats for Loyalists was changed from green to red.

By 1780, Loyalist musicians had adopted the practice of the British regiments in reversing their coat colours.

Inevitably, despite the efforts of the British to cloth their allies in a manner befitting Crown forces, many Loyalist corps were obliged to make their own arrangements for arms and clothing. Even as late as 1780, lack of proper uniforms was evident. At the action at Ransom's Mill the Patriots wore pieces of white paper in their caps while the Loyalists wore sprigs of green pine in theirs as distinctions. In this melee many of the cap devices became dislodged and a great confusion resulted with a number of combatants on both sides being mistaken for the enemy and killed by their own men.

A red cockade was generally accepted as the sign of a Tory sympathiser, all through many contemporary illustrations show black.

Many of the Tory troops of horse were clothed similar to the British Cavalry in regimental tailed coats with collar, cuffs and lapels in a facing colour and white linings. Other mounted troops wore shell jackets, either single or double breasted, with faced collar and cuffs and some-

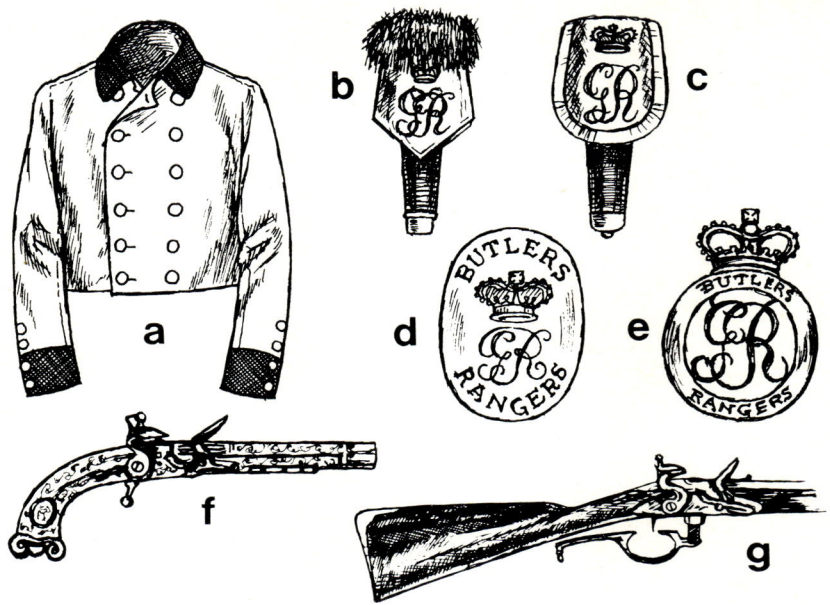

LOYALIST MISCELLANY.
a. Light Dragoon Jacket of De Lancey's Refugees.
b. Saddle holster of De Lancey's Light Dragoons.
c. Saddle holster of Emmerich's Mounted Chasseurs.
d. Belt plate of Butler's Rangers.
e. Pouch plate of Butler's Rangers.
f. One of a pair of Scottish pistols lost by Major Pitcairn,
British Marines, at Lexington. The captured pistols
were subsequently carried throughout the War
by Israel Putnam.
g. The screw plug of the Ferguson Rifle.

times with shoulder straps or cords. Numerous variations of the Light
Dragoon helmet were in use as an alternative to the cocked hat for
Cavalry. A stores list of 1778 includes blue greatcoats, helmets (with
feathers for sergeants) and chain shoulder straps. This same list gives
both leather holsters with cypher and bearskin topped holsters for
Mounted Infantry and Cavalry respectively. In 1781, red cloaks were
ordered to be provided for Provincial Cavalry.

Most accoutrements for both Loyalist horse and foot troops, such as
pouches, knapsacks, etc, were the standard British Army patterns of the
period.

Weapons were either British issue or captured stocks, although the
Loyalists of New York and New Jersey, known as the American Volunteers, were armed with the excellent Ferguson rifle, a weapon named
after its inventor, Major Patrick Ferguson, who was their commander.
The Ferguson had a screw plug at the breech which could be opened to
insert a charge by one turn of the trigger guard. It was claimed that a
soldier trained in the use of this weapon could fire six shots per minute

in a standing position. The rifle had an overall length of 52 in. (36 in. barrel length). The Ferguson was never used to the extent it might have been for two reasons. Captain Ferguson was killed at the battle of King's Mountain in 1780 before he could complete the promotion of his weapon and petty differences amongst the British High Command resulted in the project being discarded.

Regarding artillery, a number of the Loyalist corps were given light field pieces which sometimes accompanied them on campaigns.

December 30, 1777.

TEUCRO DUCE NIL DESPERANDOM.

Firſt Battalion of PENNSYLVANIA LOYALISTS, commanded by His Excellency Sir WILLIAM HOWE, K. B.

ALL INTREPID ABLE-BODIED

H E R O E S,

WHO are willing to ſerve His MAJESTY KING GEORGE the Third, in Defence of their Country, Laws and Conſtitution, againſt the arbitrary Uſurpations of a tyrannical Congreſs, have now not only an Opportunity of manifeſting their Spirit, by aſſiſting in reducing to Obedience their too-long deluded Countrymen, but alfo of acquiring the polite Accompliſhments of a Soldier, by ſerving only two Years, or during the preſent Rebellion in America.

Such ſpirited Fellows, who are willing to engage, will be rewarded at the End of the War, beſides their Laurels, with 50 Acres of Land, where every gallant Hero may retire, and enjoy his Bottle and Laſs.

Each Volunteer will receive, as a Bounty, FIVE DOLLARS, beſides Arms, Cloathing and Accoutrements, and every other Requiſite proper to accommodate a Gentleman Soldier, by applying to Lieutenant Colonel ALLEN, or at Captain KEARNY's Rendezvous, at PATRICK TONRY's, three Doors above Market-ſtreet, in Second-ſtreet.

A typical Loyalist recruiting poster, 1777.

3: Loyalist Corps

THE QUEEN'S RANGERS raised in 1776 by Robert Rogers, was commanded in 1777 first by Lieutenant Colonel French, then Major Wemys and thirdly, when Wemys was wounded, by Major John Groves Simcoe (Captain, 40th Foot Regiment). The regiment was at this time made up of eight battalion companies, one Grenadier company, one light company and one of Highlanders, complete with kilts and bagpipes.

In 1778 a Hussar troop of 30 men was formed and two years later, with Simcoe promoted to Lieutenant-Colonel of Cavalry, three troops of Light Dragoons were added to the Rangers plus a light field piece. It is not quite clear whether the 1780 addition of Light Dragoons were also clothed as Hussars or whether they were dressed in their own distinctive uniform as Lefferts suggests.

When in 1778 Loyalist regiments were ordered to change from green to red uniforms, Simcoe's efforts in retaining green coats for his Corps were successful. He maintained that green was the ideal colour for clothing light troops. His enthusiasm for Light Infantry was again reflected in 1780 when all companies of foot were given black leather light company caps to replace their white braided cocked hats. The Grenadier company retained their tall fur caps. On dress occasions feathers were worn in the caps and appear to have been combinations of

CAPS OF THE QUEEN'S RANGERS (SIMCOE'S).
a. Light Infantryman.
b. Rifleman.
c. Grenadier.

green and white, differing between companies.

The first uniform of the Infantry of the Queen's Rangers was a green coat and waistcoat. Blue was supposed to have been the facing colour but this is not certain. Contemporary water colours of the Corps painted in 1781 show the facings to be green and notes written in 1783 specify black facings. The badge of the Corps, a white metal crescent, with 'QUEEN'S RANGERS' engraved upon it was worn on the front of the cap. The following guide to the uniforms of the Corps has been compiled from contemporary evidence.

BATTALION COMPANIES (called Riflemen): Up to 1780, a cocked hat with white binding, green coats faced blue or black with pewter buttons, green waistcoats, white breeches with black linen spatterdashes in summer and brown cloth knee-length gaiters in winter. Crossbelts were black leather. After 1780 these companies changed from cocked hats to leather caps with a black feather over the top of the cap and a hackle on the left side in black with a white centre section. The crescent badge was worn on the front. If a water colour of 1781 is accurate, the Rifle companies adopted short green jackets cut square at the bottom with pewter buttons and green falldown collar and pointed cuffs. White shoulder chains are shown although these were supposed to have been worn only by Light companies. Small side pockets with flaps and three buttons may have been included on this jacket.

LIGHT COMPANIES: The same changes after 1780 as the Rifle companies but with the addition of a white metal edge to the cap. The feather over the cap was white and the hackle green with a white centre section. White breeches with black spatterdashes were worn.

GRENADIER COMPANIES: A tall cap of smooth fur with white cap lines and tassels and a hackle, green, white, black from the base was worn. The coat was green lined white with green lapels, collar and cuffs and green shoulder wings laced and edged white. The waistcoat and breeches were white and black spatterdashes were worn. Crossbelts were light brown and the musket sling was black. Lefferts shows the facings of the Grenadiers to be blue (as he does with the other Queen's Rangers). He also shows the crossbelts as black.

HUSSARS: The Hussar cap was of black cloth or felt with the crescent badge and a green bag with white tassel hanging on the left. The coat was green single-breasted with perhaps a double row of buttons and with long skirts lined white. The collar, pointed cuffs and shoulder straps were green as were the waistcoat and breeches. The shoulder sword belt and short boots were black leather. The saddle cloth was dark green with white crescents on front and rear and the saddle holsters had black fur covers.

LIGHT DRAGOONS: A black leather helmet with bearskin crest and either a green turban or one with blue and green triangles (Lefferts) and a green over white hackle. A green jacket similar to that of the Light Infantry and with shoulder chains. White or buff breeches with black boots and a metal hilted sabre on black shoulder belt. Sergeants were identified by white braiding around the collar and pointed cuffs.

The Colours of the Queen's Rangers were as follows:

THE KING'S COLOUR: The Union flag with a red shield edged gold

a. *King's Colour, The Queen's Rangers.*
b. *Regimental Colour, The Queen's Rangers.*

bearing the title, 'QUEEN'S RANGERS 1st AMERN.' in gold. The shield was surmounted by a crown in gold and crimson and flanked by two sprigs of roses and thistles in natural colours.

THE REGIMENTAL COLOUR: Blue with the same device in the centre and the small Union in the first canton.

The Queen's Rangers were a much respected Corps and admired throughout the whole of the Army for their efficiency and discipline. During the War they repeatedly defeated much larger forces of Patriot troops.

Another active Loyalist Corps was **DE LANCEY'S BRIGADE.** The men were recruited by Oliver De Lancey from New York state (New York, West Chester, King's and Queen's Counties). The scheme was to form three battalions of 500 men each and clothe them, not in Loyalist green, but in British red uniforms. The red coats had plain dark blue facings, and white linings with pewter buttons. Waistcoats and breeches were also white and black spatterdashes were worn. The cocked hats were bound with broad white lace. The only distinctions between the three battalions were the numbers and positioning of the coat buttons:

Ten equidistant on each lapel for the 1st Battalion.
Ten set in twos on each lapel for the 2nd Battalion.
Nine set in threes on each lapel for the 3rd Battalion.

In 1777 the men were issued with white linen overalls for summer wear and brown cloth overalls and a leather cap for winter wear. It is not clear whether all the companies or only the Light troops wore this cap which had a black leather front plate with a brass edge and the GR cypher and crown. The words, 'DE LANCEY' were painted in white along the bottom of the front plate.

Officers are reputed to have worn silver hat cords and button loop, silver epaulettes, gorget and belt plate with buttons arranged like those of the men. On duty officers wore crimson waist sashes and carried fusils. If the men were dressed in breeches, stockings and spatterdashes then the officers wore the same. When the men wore overalls, boots were worn by commissioned ranks.

CAPS OF LOYALIST SOLDIERS.
a. Butler's Rangers.
b. De Lancey's Brigade.
c. Light Dragoon of De Lancey's Refugees.

Another famous Loyalist corps, not to be confused with the previous one but bearing the same name, was **DE LANCEY'S REFUGEES.** This Corps was raised in 1777 and passed from the command of a Major Barmore to that of Colonel James De Lancey. The Refugees comprised seven companies of Infantry and four Light Dragoon troops which served throughout the War in and around West Chester County, New York. The Dragoons were recruited from the best families in the area and were also known as the 'Cow Boys' because of their duties in bringing live-stock to the British Army around New York.

The uniform of the Refugees was a green regimental coat with white facings, waistcoat and breeches. Cocked hats and brown cloth leggings were worn. Although the foot companies retained this dress throughout the War the Cavalry was re-equipped in 1780 as befitted Light Dragoons with the issue of leather helmets with bearskin crests, mid-blue turbans and black rosettes, short green jackets with black collar and round cuffs and British Light Dragoon equipment. The saddle holsters were fur covered and bore the Royal cypher and crown on the flap.

Records indicate that this Corps was much respected for its strict discipline and accomplished drill.

A well disciplined body of Loyalists who served alongside De Lancey's Refugees was the Corps of Colonel Andreas Emmerich known as **EMMERICH'S CHASSEURS.** Raised in 1776 it comprised a Musketeer company, a Rifle company and a Light Dragoon troop. The uniform of the Infantry was a green coat faced mid-blue with white linings, waistcoat and breeches and pewter buttons. The cocked hat had a black cockade with silver button. The mounted troops were clothed similarly but with green waistcoats. Both foot and horse wore knee-length gaiters. The Light Dragoons wore a carbine belt over their left shoulder whereas the Infantry wore the usual white or buff crossbelts. The saddle holsters had rounded flaps bearing the Royal crown and cipher in gilt. A blue cape was carried rolled behind the saddle and the sabre was usually worn from a waistbelt.

Sir John Johnson's Loyalists raised in 1776 are said to have been known to the Patriots as **THE ROYAL GREENS** as their first regimental coats were supposed to have been green faced and lined white. (Although a coat taken from Johnson's house by Patriots in 1776 was reported to have had red facings.) Buttons were pewter stamped 'R.P.' for Royal Provincials'. Breeches and waistcoats were white and the cocked hat was edged with white tape. Brown cloth knee-length gaiters were worn. The Light companies wore small green cloth shoulder wings laced with white.

In 1778 the Greens were re-organised as 'The King's Royal Regiment of New York' also known as The Queen's Loyal Americans. As a Royal regiment Johnson's were now issued with a red coat faced blue with buttons marked 'K.R.R.' inside a wreath surmounted by a crown and with 'NEW YORK' below. Officers wore gold lace on the lapels and cuffs with gold fringed epaulettes and gilt buttons. Examples of two types of officers' waistcoat exist; one of white cloth and one of scarlet cloth with gilt buttons. The latter was probably worn on dress occasions. Commissioned ranks wore white breeches with boots.

Raised by Colonel John Butler in New York in 1777, **BUTLER'S RANGERS** were an efficient and dedicated Loyalists corps. Butler was instructed by Sir George Clinton to raise eight companies each consisting of one captain, one lieutenant, three sergeants, two corporals and 50 men. It was intended to recruit for the Corps men acquainted with the language and customs of the Indians who were to work with the Rangers. These men were to form two of the eight companies. The remaining companies would be made up of men who were familiar with woodland and frontier warfare methods. The two 'Indian' companies were to be paid four shillings a man per day, twice the amount of the other six companies. All were clothed at their own expense. The first company was ready by December, 1777. Exactly one year later fully six companies had been formed and another was added in 1781. As some of the expeditions of Butler's Rangers involved covering a large area of operations many of the men were often mounted and frequently took with them two light field pieces. In winter these guns were drawn on sledges.

The uniform of the Rangers consisted of a dark green coat faced and lined red and with a dark green waistcoat. As most of their engagements were fought in the Indian manner their usual breeches and stockings were often replaced by buckskin Indian leggings or leather waist-length overalls. The head-dress of the Corps was a distinctive one, being a black leather helmet with a brass front plate embossed with a crown and the 'G.R.' cipher. Around the top of the plate, following the curve, was the word, 'BUTLER'S' and along the bottom the word, 'RANGERS'. The helmet had a black leather cockade attached to the left side. Crossbelts of buff leather were worn, having an oval belt plate which also bore the regimental cipher. A variation of this plate also decorated the flap of the cartridge pouch.

The officers wore either the leather helmet or a gold laced cocked hat. (Butler's son, Walter, an officer in the Corps was said to be wearing a black cocked hat when he was killed in action.)

Butler's Rangers acquitted themselves extremely well throughout the War, often outwitting the Patriot backwoodsmen at their own game. At the cessation of hostilities the Corps retired to Canada forming a settlement at Niagara. Their devoted Tory sympathies were again in evidence when numerous ex-Rangers flocked again to the British Colours to fight in the War of 1812.

LOYALIST CAVALRY (From contemporary sources).
a. A trooper from a water-colour of Germantown.
    Simcoe's Legion was present at this engagement and this
    may be a Light Dragoon of this Corps. (Brass helmet edged
    with fur and with red horsehair crest, green coat faced
    white with black edging, white breeche's and
    waistcoat, black boots. Red cloak over white fur holsters).
b. A Loyalist from the Graham painting of the burial of
    General Fraser, killed at Saratoga. (Green jacket with
    all white trim, white breeches and stockings with black
    half-gaiters or boots. Brass hilted sword on black belt).
c. Horseman from a print of the Battle of Camden.
    (White jacket and breeches, collar and cuffs in facing colour
    of a mid tone, black belts and boots. Some manner of
    epaulette is shown. The leather helmet has a brass band
    and peak and a transverse horsehair crest).
    Tarleton's Legion are reputed to have worn white
    during the Southern campaign.

THE BRITISH LEGION was another Loyalist corps active in partisan fighting during the Revolution. It was composed of Loyal Americans commanded by a British officer, Lieutenant Colonel Banastre Tarleton. The Legion comprised both Cavalry and Infantry with the latter often being mounted for raiding purposes.

The uniform of an officer of Legion Cavalry is clearly shown in the portrait of Tarleton by Sir Joshua Reynolds. It consists of a short green jacket with black collar and cuffs. Gold lace is evident around the collar, cuffs, front of the jacket and pockets. Two gold loops are stitched to the shoulders, the right one holding in place a black sword belt. The front of the jacket has four closely set rows of gilt buttons. Two more gilt buttons are set on each sleeve above the cuff. Buckskin breeches and kneeboots complete the uniform and the sabre has a yellow metal hilt. The head-dress worn by Tarleton in the portrait is in fact the helmet which bears his name. It consists of a black leather peaked cap with bearskin crest and having a green turban and feather. There is some controversy concerning this helmet. Opinions differ as to whether the Tarleton cap was worn by the Legion during the War or whether the Colonel wore it for his portrait (which was completed after the war) because it was then the fashionable military head-dress. The first mention of this type of helmet in England is in Inspection Returns of 1780.

Other Loyalist and Patriot Cavalry wore similar leather helmets and the green turban and feather in the portrait do suggest Loyalist colours. Another painting of an officer who served under Tarleton exists, and this shows the same type of helmet worn with a green jacket with black facings. Engravings showing Cavalry of the British Legion made some 50 years after the War show their helmet as being a black leather cap with a metal band in place of the turban and metal peak and with either a horsehair crest or fur tail placed transversely across the helmet.

The rank and file of Legion Cavalry wore a jacket similar to that of the officers but having white lace in place of gold. In the Reynolds portrait a trooper is shown in the background. He also wears a bearskin crested cap.

The Infantry of the Legion wore, according to a clothing list of 1780, green coats (probably faced black), white waistcoat and breeches, and cocked hats. Drummers are said to have worn green waistcoats and breeches but no mention is made of the regulation reversed coat colours for musicians. One chronicler states that in the Southern campaign the Legion was clad in white but this was probably because the regimental coats were discarded due to the heat and the men fought in their white waistcoats.

As with the Patriots many of the uniform details of the numerous Loyalist regiments raised have faded into obscurity. Some records how-ever do exist of a number of corps. The following list gives some basic information about them. Small clothes would be either white or buff with perhaps cloth or buckskin overalls being worn in place of breeches, while supplementary equipment such as belts, knapsacks and the like would usually be British issue.

THE ROYAL FENCIBLE AMERICANS: Red coats faced black with white lace.

THE KING'S AMERICAN DRAGOONS: Short red coats faced blue with white lace and either a bearskin crested cap or one with metal fittings and a horsehair crest.

THE NEW YORK VOLUNTEERS: Green coats, waistcoats and breeches and cocked hats (bound with white lace for sergeants). After 1780 this Corps became the 3rd American Regiment when their regimentals were changed to red coats faced buff.

1st INDEPENDENT CO. OF NEW YORK RANGERS: Short red coats with blue lapels and cuffs, and capes lined white. (Cape, in this case would refer to the collar of the coat.) Black hats with a black feather.

THE LOYAL QUEEN'S COUNTY REGIMENT: Raised in 1777 consisted of 17 Foot companies and three troops of Light Dragoons.

The description of a Foot officer's uniform is given as a scarlet coat faced blue and lined white with white waistcoat and breeches, silver buttons and epaulettes, a cocked hat with silver edging lace, button and loop. The rank and file would probably wear white hat tape and a similar uniform.

KING'S CAROLINA RANGERS: Short green coats with plain green lapels and crimson collar and cuffs.

ROYAL NORTH CAROLINA VOLUNTEERS: Red coats with plain blue facings.

SOUTH CAROLINA LOYALISTS: Red coats with red lapels and collar and cuffs yellow. White lacing.

MARYLAND LOYALISTS: Red coats faced olive green and laced white.

PENNSYLVANIA LOYALISTS: Red coats faced olive green and laced white.

PRINCE OF WALES' AMERICAN REGIMENT: Red coats faced blue laced white.

THE LOYAL AMERICAN REGIMENT: Red coats with plain buff facings.

KING'S AMERICAN REGIMENT OR ASSOCIATED REFUGEES: Red coats faced olive green with white buttonhole lace. This regiment later became the 4th American.

NOVA SCOTIA VOLUNTEERS: Red coats with plain green lapels.

GUIDES AND PIONEERS: Short red coats with red lapels, black collar and cuffs and Light Infantry cap.

GARRISON BATTALIONS: Red coats with green collar and cuffs and white lace.

1st, 2nd and 3rd NEW JERSEY VOLUNTEERS: Red coats faced blue, the regiments being distinguished by having white laced buttonholes spaced singly, in twos and in threes respectively. (Similar to De Lancey's Brigade.)

THE KING'S ORANGE RANGERS: Red coats faced bright yellow and laced white.

Appendix 1: Bibliography of Reference Sources

THE following books and papers, many now unobtainable, give useful source material for a further study of the subject.

ARMY OF THE USA, by H. A. Ogden.

UNIFORMS OF THE AMERICAN REVOLUTION, by Lefferts.

SOLDIERS OF THE AMERICAN ARMY, by Kredel and Todd.

COPIES OF MILITARY COLLECTOR AND HISTORIAN.

HISTORY OF THE UNITED STATES AND ITS PEOPLES, by E. M. Avery.

PICTORIAL HISTORY OF THE AMERICAN REVOLUTION, by Robert Sears.

HISTORY OF THE UNITED STATES FLAG, by Prebble.

LIBRARY OF CONGRESS PAPERS.

REGIMENTAL COLOURS IN THE WAR OF THE REVOLUTION, by G. Davis.

CONTEMPORARY CLOTHING LISTS, PRINTS AND PAINTINGS.

Appendix 2: Formations and Organisation

WHILE actual detailed drill and tactics of the War of Independence period is beyond the scope of this book it is of interest to show the composition of regiments and how they were formed up in fighting order. This is done in diagrammatic form in this section.

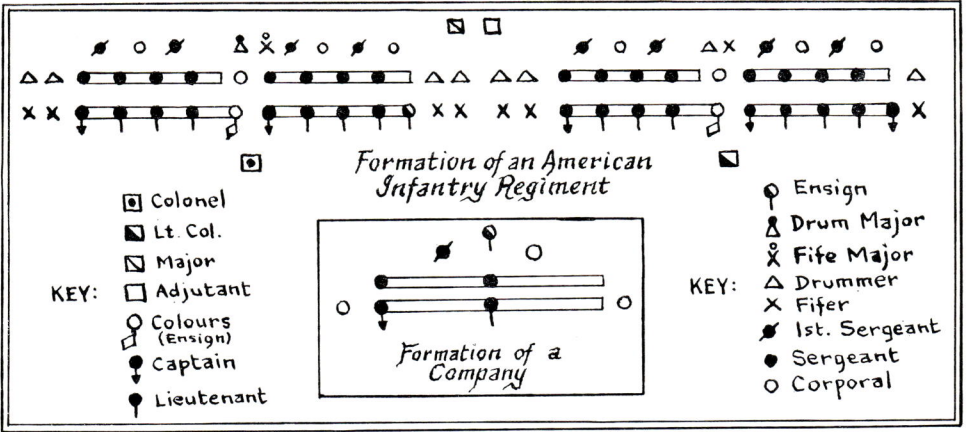

Each field officer, besides his other duties commanded a company. Left to right in the diagram above, the eight companies of a regiment were commanded in the following order: (1) First Captain's; (2) Colonel's; (3) Fourth Captain's; (4) Major's; (5) Third Captain's; (6) Lieutenant-Colonel's; (7) Fifth Captain's; (8) Second Captain's. Details are taken from Steuben's Regulations.

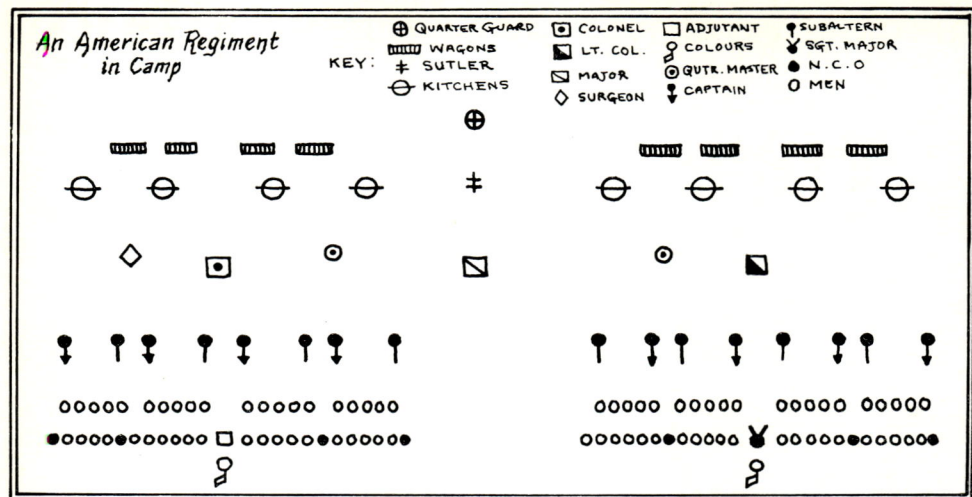

(Details from Steuben's Regulations)

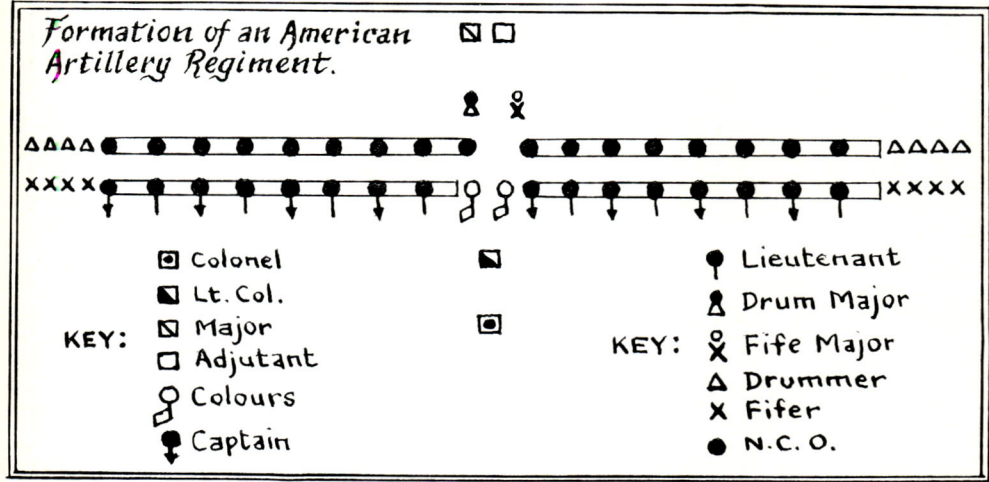

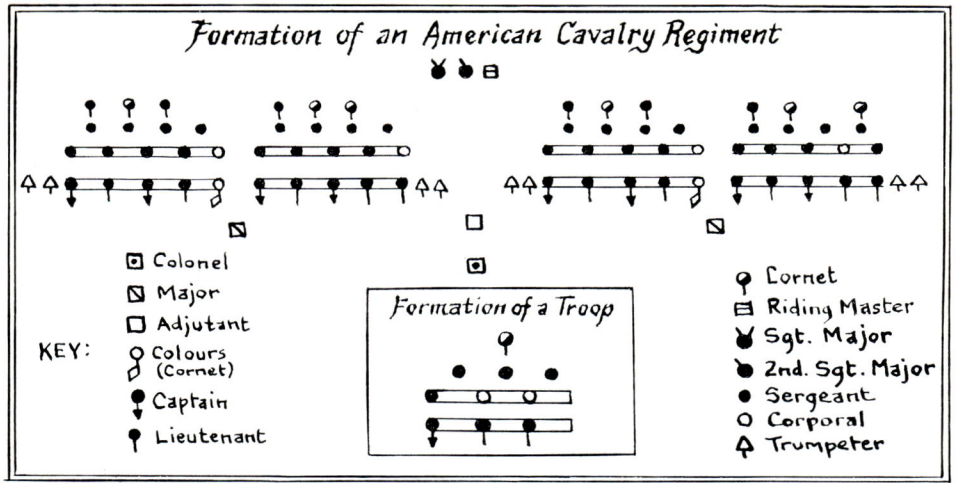

(Details from Steuben's Regulations)

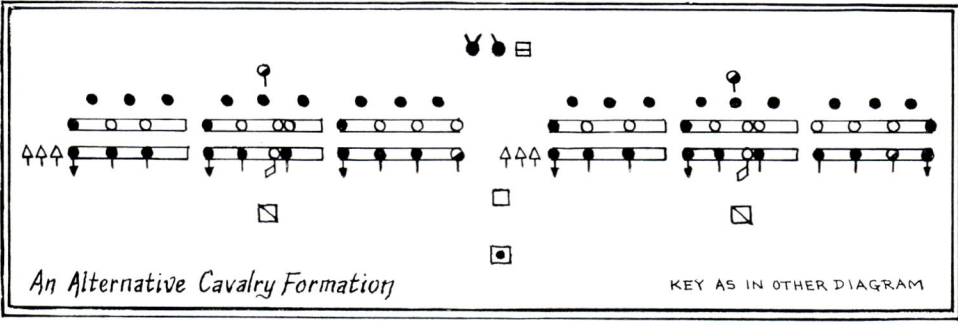

Notes